Questions

GOD

Asks Us

PAULA PATTON QUINN

TREATY OAK PUBLISHERS

PUBLISHER'S NOTE

This is a work of personal memoir and inspiration. All of the characters, business establishments, and events are based on the author's personal experiences. Individuals' names may have been changed to protect their privacy.

Printed and published in the United States of America

TREATY OAK PUBLISHERS

ISBN: 978-1-943658-54-1

DEDICATION

To Michael, my true companion.

Congratulations to the reader who finds this book! Paula Quinn has prepared a feast in the presence of the Lord. I am so grateful she did the work and invited us to the table. I broke from my usual habit of binge reading to take this book slow. Boy, am I glad I did! Meditating on the questions God wants to ask us today resulted in new understanding of God's affection for me personally. Wow!

Cathy Krafve,
Host of Fireside Talk Radio, Author of
The Well: *The Art of Drawing Out Authentic Conversations*

"Questions God Asks Us is a fresh and engaging approach to the ancient Christian art of lectio divina. With the gentle honesty of a faithful friend and the keen insight of a spiritual guide, Paula Quinn invites us into a deeper relationship with God. When we listen attentively to the questions God asks us in Scripture, we see more clearly who God is, who we are, and who God calls us to be. If you hunger to experience the living God, who is always and everywhere present, then this is a book to be pondered and practiced."

The Rev. Kelly Koonce,
Episcopal Priest, Spiritual Director, and Grief Educator

"Paula Quinn has tackled difficult subjects in a down-to-earth way. Her take on what questions God might ask us shed a spiritual, yet very human, light on how we can change the way we go about our daily lives."

Honorable Pamela Williford
Former US Ambassador to Switzerland

"The perspective that Paula Quinn brings to the idea of conversations with God is personal and yet available to all of us. Even getting to know a human being in depth is a serious thing for those of us who believe each person is unique and has value. God know us and wants us to know aand trust Him. That is at the heart of this book.

Bishop William Millsaps
Presiding Bishop of The Episcopal Missionary Church,
Bishop of the Diocese of the South (EMC),
and Rector of Christ Church, Monteagle, TN

But I lavish unfailing love
for a thousand generations
on those who love me and
obey my commands.

Exodus 20:6
New Living Translation

All scriptures citations are from the *New International Version Bible* unless otherwise indicated.

INTRODUCTION

When I was fifteen I had an encounter with God. It came about while I prayed just by myself. It was not a conversion because I was already a Christian. Nor was it a confession, because at fifteen my list of transgressions wasn't long, but I was definitely searching. I was seeking God, but also holding him at arm's length. I wasn't sure I really wanted him more than I wanted to be in charge of my own agenda.

This impasse lasted for months when, at last, on one ordinary day I asked God to come into my life. His response was so overwhelming, my sense of his presence was so palpable, that it changed me forever. This book arises out of that first experience of God's presence, my love of scripture and my ongoing walk with Jesus. The idea of the book, however, came after an experience many years ago.

Twenty years ago I attended a quiet day retreat at my church during Lent. The retreat leader gave us the opportunity to reflect on a series of questions posed by God to different people in the scriptures. I remember choosing two questions and answering them as though God had asked me the question himself. I found the exercise so interesting and meaningful that I've continued to pay attention to the questions whenever I came across one.

In many cases, the questions show that God not only had conversations with all sorts of people, he had relationships with them. Many of us want this connection, and I believe God wants this as well. If we are interested in a closer relationship with God, then thinking about and answering these questions, as if God posed them to us, might be a way to spend intimate time with him. After all, God did not start out in a temple or a cathedral. He started his relationship with us without any of the trappings of religion. He first spoke to us in a garden. He met with our ancestors in the cool of the day. His questions can be a vehicle for us to spend the same kind of intimate time with God.

In the format of this book, I provide the question God asks, the scriptural context, and my own reflections. Before you look at the context or read my commentary, sit with the question and see what thoughts or answers first come to your mind. I hope my reflections will serve as a catalyst for your own thoughts, and you may well come up with very different ideas. If we had the opportunity to be face to face I would say, "Here's what this makes me think about. What about you?" You will have an opportunity to meditate on the question, on further questions that the original question suggests, and on a few additional verses from scripture.

I encourage you to read the questions and the accompanying scriptures as lectio divina. They are divine questions; lectio divina—an ancient form of slow, attentive, reflective, and meditative reading—treats scripture as God's living word to us. It's not an academic study; rather it's a personal engagement with the word and with God. Think of it as having a personal conversation with God where the scripture suggests the topic.

The practice involves four stages: reading, meditation, prayer and contemplation. Allow the words and the promptings of the Spirit to speak to you, as you allow the Holy Spirit to commune with your spirit. Some questions will resonate deep within, others might lead your heart in a surprising direction.

The questions are an invitation to you to reflect on your journey, as well as your memories and relationships, and to share your thoughts and feelings with God. It's also an opportunity to listen to God, both in his written word and in your heart.

When you read the questions God asked, hear God asking you these questions, in your particular circumstances. Sit with the question for awhile and notice what comes to mind. You might journal your thoughts and provide your own answer. Some questions might take more time; you might come back to them over the course of several days, or circle back to them after several months. Others may not touch you right away; hold on to them for a later time. After you answer the question, allow a few minutes of silence before the Lord. It's always possible that God will speak to you, and to be still before him is often helpful. Consider each question as something God is asking you.

Here are some ways to get started. First consider the question by itself and note your first thoughts. You'll also find a story around the questions. What experience of God did the person in the Biblical account have that speaks to your circumstances, relationships, fears, or hopes? What does their encounter reveal to you about God or about yourself? Does their story open up your own memories or affect the way you understand the question?

This book can also be used in a group study or a retreat setting. It can be completed and picked up again after time has passed. Our answers can change because our lives change. I hope the questions open up wonderful conversations and a deeper connection between you and God. I hope these stories cast fresh light on your own story. One of the descriptions of God in the Bible is "Counselor." The questions—and our attempt to answer them—provide much food for thought. Sometimes it takes awhile to see what God might really be trying to ask us. The process can lead to a dialogue with God, just like the people in the accounts. They can provide an opportunity to know the "Wonderful Counselor" (*Isaiah 9:6*) of our souls. The interactions can be divine therapy.

TABLE OF CONTENTS

III. MOSES, THE FRIEND OF GOD
Questions 14-19

IV. THE BEGINNING OF THE NATION
Questions 20-26

V. THE PROPHETS
Questions 27-34

VI. THE PROPHETS IN RELATIONSHIP WITH GOD
Questions 35-40

VII. Epilogue

Acknowledgements

Questions

GOD

Asks Us

FIRST FAMILY

Chapters 1-8

God comes to meet with his first children, Adam and Eve, in the cool of the day. Much action, all of creation, in fact, has been required to lay the groundwork for God's ultimate masterpiece, his children. Who knows how many questions and conversations passed before these first recorded questions in scripture, but these questions reveal the intimate relationship—the normal, everyday relationship—that Adam and Eve enjoyed with God.

They also reveal God's reaction to their choices and their reaction to him. They remind us of the relationship between parents and children. They are not about theology or what to believe in or the law. In the beginning there was one "law."

To recap the story: Adam and Eve were born into a delightful garden, surrounded by beauty. All kinds of trees were planted there, including the tree of life, but they were forbidden to eat from one tree since the fruit was deadly: the tree of knowledge of good and evil.

We're not sure how long Adam and Eve enjoyed their lovely garden, taking care of the plants, naming the animals, and walking with God, but at some point a serpent entered the scene. Before long, he had Adam and Eve eating out of the palm of his hand.

How did he do this? He told Eve that far from bringing death, the fruit from the tree of knowledge of good and evil will make her wise, this fruit will open her eyes, she will be like God. He insinuated this was the reason God had forbidden them to eat the fruit from this tree, because God was holding out on them. He convinced Eve this was the very fruit she must eat in order to have what she didn't even know she wanted. She needed something more in order to feel special, and neither Adam or Eve seemed to remember the truth: they were already "like" God, already created in his image. They both succumbed to Satan's ploy.

Doesn't this temptation resonate with us to this very day?

Before you begin Chapter I, take a few moments to meditate on "family," the starting point for all of us. In the beginning it seems God was very much a part of the human family. You might contemplate what role, if any, God played in your family of origin. Our parents, siblings, and our extended family set the stage for us. They are our first teachers. We learn from them, for better or worse, who we are, what our place is, and what is possible. Wherever we are on our journey, we must reckon with this starting point.

Chapter 1

Where are you?

Now the serpent was craftier than any of the wild animals the Lord God had made. He said to the woman, "Did God really say, 'You must not eat from any tree in the garden?'"

The woman said to the serpent, "We may eat from the trees in the garden, but God did say, 'You must not eat fruit from the tree that is in the middle of the garden, and you must not touch it or you will die.'"

"You will not surely die," the serpent said to the woman. "For God knows that when you eat of it your eyes will be opened, and you will be like God, knowing good and evil."

When the woman saw that the fruit of the tree was good for food and pleasing to the eye, and also desirable for gaining wisdom, she took some and ate it. She also gave some to her husband, who was with her and he ate it. Then the eyes of both of them were opened, and they realized they were naked; so they sewed fig leaves together and made coverings for themselves.

Then the man and his wife heard the sound of the Lord God as he was walking in the garden in the cool of the day, and they hid from the Lord God among the trees of the garden. But the Lord God called to the man, "Where are you?"

Genesis 3:1-9

God came walking in the garden in the cool of the day, calling out for his children. The scene evokes the best of family rituals: coming together after a long day of work or school to share the day, husbands and wives greeting each other, parents hugging their children. The story has the feeling that this was God's routine, that he regularly stopped by for a chat in the breezy, cool evening.

In the story, Adam and Eve heard God coming and recognized his approach. He called for them as he likely had before, only this time they ran for cover. They didn't run to greet him because now they were filled with fear and shame.

So God asked the first recorded question, "Where are you?"

The question is a harbinger of many questions to follow because we don't get rid of fear and shame with ease. What lies ahead is a long history of running away and hiding. God's question invited Adam and Eve to come out, to come clean, and talk to him. They didn't have to search for God; he came looking for them.

Their impulse to hide went hand-in-hand with their violation of the one rule of Eden. This urge seems to be written into our very being, into the structure of our DNA: do wrong, then cover up. Children do this without anyone teaching them how. They may be rather transparent about it in the beginning, but by the time they are adults, they get very good at the covering-up and hiding game. They—we—learn to hide in plain sight.

We hide in a myriad of ways. We put on a happy face when really we are depressed. We go along with the crowd even if it makes us uncomfortable. We join Adam and Eve in the dark shrubbery because we too are overcome by shame and fear.

God calls, "Where are you?"

On bad days we isolate. We pull the covers over our heads. We sabotage a relationship because we're afraid of getting hurt. Our anxieties get the better of us and we numb ourselves with alcohol or prescriptions or both.

God calls, "Where are you?"

Our authentic self goes underground and we don't even know it. We remember something painful from our childhood. We never told a soul, or we did tell, and the telling made it worse. Or we suffered a deep hurt, a heartbreak we believe can never be healed. We vow never to let that happen again. We disconnect from our own hearts.

And God calls. We can be oblivious to his call, and we might not know that sometimes he says, "Where is the real you?"

Not long ago, while praying, I had a vision of Jesus standing behind a white fence, the kind of fence you see on a farm. He called me to walk around the fence and stand by him. When I did, I looked up at a rolling pasture and a scene from my child-hood came to me. I was riding horses with my friends. I real-ized that, as much fun as I had with those girls, I didn't quite fit in. Jesus said he knew how I felt, he was with me then, he had always been with me. When I first lived that scene, I was not conscious God was anywhere around, much less that he noticed me. Where are you? When I was a girl, I laughed with my friends, but also tried to fit in. I felt like I was on my own, but on the day of my prayer as I witnessed this scene, I stood on the same side of the fence with Jesus.

There's another way to think about this first question. Jesus told a story about a shepherd with one hundred sheep. One goes astray. The shepherd searches night and day for just that one. All the while I imagine him calling out for that sheep by name, even singing out, "Where are you?" The shepherd was overjoyed to find his sheep and carry him back home.

In a funny way, this story is familiar to me. Several years ago I had a dog that was an escape artist. She loved nothing more than to get her companion, our other dog, and roam the neighborhood together for hours. I waited by the phone in hopes someone would find them and call my number on their dog tags. Or I would set out in my car searching for them. On any given day you could call my house and hear the message, "I'm out looking for my dogs. If you've found them, please let me know and I'll come and get them right away." I never failed to search for them. I knew about traffic and dognappers and animal control. I knew about danger. I always searched for them because they were my dogs, and I loved them.

How would you respond if, in your hiding place, the place you are trying to fit in, your day to day life, your obscurity, you remembered that God is in love with you? How would you feel, who would you be, if you were mired in guilt and God came looking for you, if you heard him calling your name?

Even if you often meet with him, would it make a difference if you believed that God is looking forward to it and calling out to you in particular? Maybe you used to walk with God in the cool of the day, but not for a while and who knows why? Or perhaps you yearn for this kind of intimacy. God asks, "Where are you?"

Prayer

Father,

It's comforting to know that you come seeking me; it is truly what I want. To know I'm included and I belong means everything to me. I want to walk with you in the cool of the day. I want to slow down long enough to really connect with you. I want it to be as real as talking to my husband or my mother or my best friend. Thank you for coming to me.

Amen

Please take an opportunity now to be still before the Lord. Then in a journal or notebook, write down your thoughts as you meditate on the question "Where are you?" Maybe later read the questions in "Further Reflections" and the scripture in "Lectio Divina" and journal your thoughts.

Spend a few minutes in quiet contemplation. Listen for the Holy Spirit and speak from your heart to God. Take a few minutes to listen or share the silence in the presence of God.

Where are you?

Further Reflections

1. When you ponder this question, do you hear an angry tone in God's voice or a tone of happy anticipation?

2. How would you respond if you really believed (or remembered) that God looks forward to spending time with you?

Lectio Divina

Ezekiel 34:11-12

For this is what the Sovereign Lord says: I myself will search for my sheep and look after them. As a shepherd looks after his scattered flock when he is with them, so I will look after my sheep. I will rescue them from all the places where they were scattered on a day of clouds and darkness.

Song of Songs 3:2

I will get up now and go about the city, through its streets and squares; I will search for the one my heart loves.

Chapter 2

Who told you that you were naked?

He answered, "I heard you in the garden, and I was afraid because I was naked and so I hid." And he said, "Who told you that you were naked?"

Genesis 3:10-11a

Adam and Eve were made for each other. After God pronounced them "one flesh," they stood together in innocent union. "The man and his wife were both naked and felt no shame" (*Genesis 2:25*). We can assume they felt no fear either. Before Adam and Eve ate the fruit, before they broke trust with God, their nakedness was the most natural thing in the world. Afterward, this natural state was to be hidden and covered. It turned out the fruit—the fruit the serpent promised would open their eyes—at once caused them to see their own nakedness in an ugly light. Now they were naked, frightened, and ashamed. Maybe this was what the serpent had wanted all along.

What is it to be naked? For Adam and Eve, it was to be exposed, to be vulnerable, weak, self-conscious, and embarrassed. Feeling these things was so uncomfortable that Adam and Eve took the first things at hand, some fig leaves, and covered up with them. We've been covering our weaknesses, insecurities, vulnerability, shame, and guilt ever since.

As you consider this question—"Who told you that you were naked?"—think about the implications of why and when you want to cover up. Keep in mind, we all find a lot of ways to cover up. Here are some favorites besides clothes: cars, houses, résumés, degrees, achievements, awards, jewelry, bank accounts, good works, and charity. None of these is bad and they aren't necessarily cover-ups, but they certainly can be.

We also use blame, anger, manipulation, charm, and religion. At a minimum we can use these things to distract others from seeing our true selves: "Look at all I have… Don't see my nakedness... I've worked so hard... Look at my accomplishments... Look at my house, my beautiful children, my success... I must be special." Remember the story, "The Emperor's New Clothes"? He parades around naked, believing he's wearing the latest fashion. He even convinces many of the townspeople until a little boy points out the truth. The story resonates because we all do it, or we know someone else who does.

God asked who did this to them, who caused this shame, who told them they were naked. Of course, he already knew their eating the fruit triggered this sad turn of affairs. Although the serpent didn't have to tell them they were naked, he too must have suspected or hoped this would be the consequence. The question indicated that God wanted them to identify the culprit.

Has anyone done this to you, caused you to feel uncovered and ashamed? When have you desperately tried to cover up? Maybe someone has outed you, seen through your cover, and pointed out the very things that cause you the most doubt about yourself.

I remember the first time I felt shame. I was nine years old, in the fourth grade, and I got into a scuffle on the playground. One of the boys grabbed my hands, twisted them, and wouldn't let go. Being a feisty girl, I leaned down and bit his wrist. No blood. No teeth marks. Not even a fight, but someone reported it all to the teacher. Back in the classroom she told me, in front of everyone, that I had acted like an uncivilized savage for biting someone. I was so embarrassed I put my head on my desk and cried. I wanted to be invisible.

This same teacher often broke rulers over Bobby Knight and Paul Fizan whenever they got a spelling word wrong. The worst thing she did was to my classmate Theresa. One day she saw, written in lipstick on the bathroom mirror, "Theresa loves Mike." The teacher yanked Theresa out of her desk and led her out of the classroom with these words, "Fool's names, like fool's faces, always seen in public places."

A lot of us suffered through that pretty humiliating year. She pointed out our flaws and mistakes for all to see. For years, I cringed whenever I remembered her words. (I'm thinking Bobby, Paul, and Theresa did, too.) A long time passed before it occurred to me how wrong she was to have done those things.

Back to the scene in the garden. Adam and Eve came out of the bushes with their fig leaves in place, but God didn't leave them in this inadequate outfit. He knew, despite the love and goodness of their original state, they now needed a cover, or at least they believed they did. He did not leave them hiding in shame. He made them proper clothing out of animal skins, a sacrifice of a good creature on behalf of his beloved children.

God never forgot the shame and nakedness of his first children. When he sent his own beloved son to us, part of his mission was to die on a cross: naked, weak, vulnerable, and exposed to all the world. He identified with all of us. God himself, naked, weak, and vulnerable.

Prayer

Father,

Sometimes I've devised a cover for getting by in the world. And in all honesty sometimes I feel you are not to be trusted. Because I so want the life I have crafted, my private prescriptions for my own nakedness, I'm jittery about what you might have in mind.

But when I see you loving me, creating a proper "outfit" for me, the desire to lay down my mask is so sweet. The weariness of holding that mask in place can be overwhelming.

Thank you that you accept me and love me, because you want my light to shine.

Amen

Please take an opportunity now to be still before the Lord. Then in a journal or notebook, write down your thoughts as you meditate on the question "Who told you that you were naked?" Maybe later read the questions in "Further Reflections" and the scripture in "Lectio Divina" and journal your thoughts.

Spend a few minutes in quiet contemplation. Listen for the Holy Spirit and speak from your heart to God. Take a few minutes to listen or share the silence in the presence of God.

Who told you that you were naked?

Further Reflections

1. When did you first experience nakedness or shame? Who was involved?

2. What makes you feel most vulnerable and what "costume" do you use for a cover-up?

Lectio Divina

Isaiah 61:10
> I delight greatly in the Lord;
> my soul rejoices in my God.
> For he has clothed me with garments of salvation
> and arrayed me in a robe of righteousness,
> as a bridegroom adorns his head like a priest,
> and as a bride adorns herself with her jewels.

Psalm 34:4-5
> I sought the Lord and he answered me;
> he delivered me from all my fears.
> Those who look to him are radiant;
> their faces are never covered with shame.

Chapter 3

Have you eaten from the tree I have commanded you not to eat from?

And he said, "Who told you that you were naked? Have you eaten from the tree that I commanded you not to eat from?"

Genesis 3:11

Adam and Eve clambered out of the bushes with their fig leaves in place and God said, "Did you eat the fruit I told you would be the death of you?"

Adam could have said, "Yes." Or, "The serpent came along and seduced Eve and I didn't do a thing to stop him. I didn't stick up for you or interrupt his lies. I just let it happen and then I joined in too." He could have said, "I'm so sorry. Please forgive us."

Eve could've chimed in. "It's all my fault. I listened to that slimy snake and then I talked Adam into eating some of the fruit too." Or, "I got suspicious of you. I thought you were holding out on me. I thought you were trying to keep me under your thumb." She could have said, "I see the mistake I've made. I've ruined everything. I'm miserable, please help."

But they didn't say anything like that.

Adam confessed, but then blamed Eve, "The woman you put here with me—she gave me some fruit from the tree and I ate it."

It sounds like Adam tried to shift the blame to God as well. After all, God was the one who brought Eve into the picture. Then Eve blamed the serpent.

Just a little while earlier, Adam and Eve were God's crowning gifts to each other. They were in love. They were one flesh, in unity with each other and with God. They were happy. Moreover, they had a destiny. They had a garden to tend and animals to name. They were to start a family that would over time fill the whole earth. They were to rule and reign over everything. God had blessed them.

Now they didn't trust God or each other. How could they get back their innocence?

The serpent lied. The serpent promised them that the fruit would bring wisdom. He promised they would be like God. He promised them independence.

What they got was alienation from each other and from God. They got a sense of their own inadequacy. Instead of independence, they got fear.

The serpent also promised them the fruit would open their eyes. Perhaps, but they did not like what they saw; their vision was skewed. In effect, he stole their blessing and their birthright. Their response might have been different if the serpent had invited them outright to join him in a rebellion against God, or if he had said, "Whatever you do, don't taste the fruit of the tree of life." They might have seen through such an obvious attempt at a coup. They might have resisted. But he was a crafty serpent and knew just what to say.

God's question was straightforward. "Did you do it?"

If they had just said, "Yes," what would have happened?

The difficulty we all have admitting when we do something wrong becomes a big problem. We can see hints of other problems as well. We have difficulty discerning bad fruit from good fruit, and what we think will bring us wisdom often brings confusion, strife, or regret. Instead of gaining wisdom, we often use knowledge to prove we're right. Or we say we are pursuing wisdom, but what we're really after is power. Maybe Adam and Eve thought that if they knew all that was good and all that was evil, they would always choose wisely. The choice to eat that fruit turned out to be a slippery slope.

Most serious of all the consequences: in the end, the fruit produced death. Once ingested, it became a part of them. In some mysterious way, Adam and Eve consumed something good but also something evil and dark. Knowing the tree was in the garden did not change Adam or Eve. Eating the fruit, however, put them on an irrevocable path to the grave.

The universal answer to this question—"Did you do it?"—is "yes." The template for all humanity was set. We have all eaten forbidden fruit. We all know good, but we know evil, too, as perpetrators and victims. Often we ingest fruit we don't even want, such as the fruit of anxiety or worry, or the fruit of knowledge that we think gives us the upper hand in arguments, or the right to be judgy. None of it brings life. If we try in all honesty to answer God's question, maybe that action can become a step out of our messes and toward a restored relationship with God. God's question might not be an angry scold, but rather an invitation to turn away from the thing robbing us of peace and joy and come back to him.

No matter what we have, we often yearn for more, or what someone else has, or what is forbidden, even deadly. Adam and Eve, covered with their fig leaves, argued over whose fault it was, all because they broke the one rule God gave them, all because they believed the serpent. Adam and Eve had a choice: to believe what God said or to believe what the serpent told them. It's our choice too.

Prayer

Lord,

I have lost count of how many times I have done what I thought was wise and lived to regret it, and times I too ate forbidden fruit. A few times stand out. You already know all about them. I wish I could take them back. I so wish for a clean slate. Your great promise, that you wash away every sin, every failure, all my disobedience and mistakes, is such great comfort.

Even now I ask that you undo any damage that I have caused and to somehow redeem it. I invite you to show me when I blame others and how I look for a scapegoat for problems I myself create. I repent. I cast my lot with you.

Amen

Please take an opportunity now to be still before the Lord. Then in a journal or notebook, write down your thoughts as you meditate on the question "Have you eaten from the tree I have commanded you not to eat from?" Maybe later read the questions in "Further Reflections" and the scripture in "Lectio Divina" and journal your thoughts.

Spend a few minutes in quiet contemplation. Listen for the Holy Spirit and speak from your heart to God. Take a few minutes to listen or share the silence in the presence of God.

Have you eaten from the tree I have commanded you not to eat from?

Further Reflections

1. Do you have a temptation that keeps getting the better of you?

2. What have been the consequences of eating that forbidden fruit?

Lectio Divina

1 John 1:8-9

If we claim to be without sin, we deceive ourselves and the truth is not in us. If we confess our sins, he is faithful and just and will forgive our sins and cleanse us from all unrighteousness.

Psalm 32:5 (The Passion Translation)

Then I finally admitted to you all my sins,
refusing to hide them any longer.
I said, "My life-giving God,
I will openly acknowledge my evil actions."
And you forgave me!
All at once the guilt of my sin washed away
and all my pain disappeared!

Chapter 4

What is this you have done?

The man said, "The woman you put here with me—she gave me some fruit from the tree and I ate it."

Then the Lord God said to the woman, "What is this you have done?"

Genesis 3:13

There are at least two ways to hear the question: "What is this you have done?" Both understandings depend on the motives and heart of the one asking the question.

I hear a cry of lament; someone else may hear fury. The former is the cry of a parent's heart. The cry when you discover that your precious child has made a stupid, thoughtless, short-sighted, bad, wrong choice, and in an instant you grasp the consequences and repercussions of this choice—and it is too late to take it back. There is no easy fix. It is your own cry of regret when you ruin a relationship or a reputation: "What have I done?" The cry of loss.

It's also the cry of a beloved who has been betrayed.

The question could also be an accusation. It could be the voice of a monarch confronting a rebellious subject. "What is this you have done? This is high treason! Lock her up!" Before you consider this aspect of the question, think about this: God asked what she had done and Eve right away answered that the serpent deceived her and so she ate the fruit. She didn't cower in fear or hide behind Adam. Whatever the tone of God's voice, Eve was not so alarmed that she couldn't speak or that she attempted an escape. Her quick reply is a clue about the way she heard the question.

In Eve's defense, though she blamed the snake, she also spoke the truth. She was deceived. She did admit what she'd done. This, too, feels familiar. I have been deceived, or at least manipulated. I have listened to a serpentine voice and realized it too late. I have tasted forbidden fruit, and, just like Eve, I was not force-fed.

God knew something had to be done; Adam and Eve ate fruit from a tree that released all sorts of ills and eventually death. The fruit was like taking slow poison. It was like taking a drug which was doomed from the first taste to be addictive. It was like the Turkish Delight the White Witch gave Edmund in the book by C.S. Lewis, *The Lion, the Witch, and the Wardrobe*. Edmund later betrayed all his friends and family for one more bite. Think of someone in the grip of addiction living like that forever.

There are other implications of this story. Everything God created was generative. Seed would produce fruit, and then more seeds. Cows would produce baby calves, and so on. Adam and Eve were mandated to be fruitful and fill the earth. He created the universe itself to expand. So perhaps when evil was unleashed, it too would scatter evil seeds that would take root and produce evil fruit. Evil would spread like wildfire.

Now God has a problem.

Because there was another extraordinary tree in the garden, the tree of life. Adam and Eve would have to leave Eden. If they continued eating from both trees, they would grow in the knowledge of good but that's not all. They would grow in the knowledge of evil as well—with no end in sight. For now, there would be no going back. God could not take the risk of his children eating from the tree of life in their fallen condition. Perhaps it was a kindness that God was not willing to let them live forever camped out by the tree of knowledge of good and evil, forever in the grip of fear and shame, becoming more and more fragmented with each passing year.

Even with forgiveness there are often consequences. A time would come for redemption and restoration, but God did not rush forward to that day. He didn't act like nothing happened or that it didn't matter. He cried out, "What is this you have done?" In this moment, we glimpse God's disappointment, his deep anguish, his grief for what has been lost as well as for what might have been.

We can see why God was so distressed about what they had done. It was not just a matter of their disobedience. Adam and Eve couldn't begin to answer God's question because they couldn't fathom the repercussions. But God knew. God had created them in his image. "God is one" (*Deuteronomy 6:4*). "God is light; in him there is no darkness at all" (*I John 1:5*). There is no dichotomy in God; he is pure; he is good. Created in that image, Adam and Eve had been pure too. They were "one," and there was no darkness in them. But the tree of knowledge had mixed fruit: good and evil. Once ingested, that duality took root in them. God saw that the battle between good and evil would be waged internally and externally for the rest of their lives. There would always be traces of that original image, but it would never be quite the same again.

Another far-reaching consequence would emerge. Centuries later Jesus taught that the pure in heart are blessed to "see God" (*Matthew 5:8*). This scripture points to a connection between purity and vision. Think about water that is pure—it's crystal clear, while water contaminated by pollutants or waste is murky. The fruit they ate was not pure; the good was contaminated with evil. Perhaps that impurity has affected mankind's vision of God ever since.

I offer you another way to look at it. Centuries after this encounter, God gave a revelation of himself to Moses. He tucked Moses into the cleft of a rock and passed by, proclaiming his nature: "the Lord is compassionate and gracious, slow to anger, abounding in love and faithfulness" (*Exodus 34:5-6*). This was, at least in part, their original "image." Adam and Eve could have left a legacy of grace and compassion, of being slow to anger, and a spirit of abounding love and faith. If this image was lost or tainted, no wonder God cried out, "What is this you have done?" Maybe in this moment God saw what it would cost not only Adam and Eve, but all their children yet to come. He saw what it would cost him, too, that someone he loved, who had never tasted its fruit, would be crucified on this tree.

Adam and Eve left the garden, with bravery or in fear we are not told, and walked into the wild. However, a postscript to this sad episode occurred. A hint of better days a long way off. God promised Eve that one day a child born of a woman would crush the serpent, the very one whose lies had ruined so much. God would not let the serpent get away with his treachery. Nor did God destroy the tree of life; rather, he placed angels with flaming swords to guard the way to it. And someday, millennia from then, a child born of a woman would crush the serpent and forge the way back to the holy garden and the sacred tree of life.

The question echoes in all our hearts, "What have I done?" We make choices that have long-lasting consequences. We often live with regret. We fear our future will be marred by the mistakes we've made. This question invites confession, soul-searching, brutal honesty about ourselves, and openness before God without excuses and blaming, and also trust and hope that, in spite of what we've done, he has a plan.

Prayer

Father,

I actually identify with you on this question. When my own children messed up, disobeyed, or made very foolish choices, I said these words in my heart. I grasped that there would be consequences I could not fix, and my heart was so sad for them. It was my heart of love for them at those times that shows me how much you love us all. I understand a parent's love.

My love for my children may not be as unconditional as your love is for us, but it is powerful and unrelenting. My own experience has given me a glimmer of your extraordinary love. Thank you.

Amen

Please take an opportunity now to be still before the Lord. Then in a journal or notebook, write down your thoughts as you meditate on the question "What is this you have done?" Maybe later read the questions in "Further Reflections" and the scripture in "Lectio Divina" and journal your thoughts.

Spend a few minutes in quiet contemplation. Listen for the Holy Spirit and speak from your heart to God. Take a few minutes to listen or share the silence in the presence of God.

What is this you have done?

Further Reflections

1. What have you lost as a result of deception?

2. How do you deal with your own knowledge of good and evil?

3. What serpent has slithered into your life? Did you recognize it for what it was?

Lectio Divina

Matthew 13:24
The kingdom of heaven is like a man who sowed good seed in his field. But while everyone was sleeping, his enemy came and sowed weeds among the wheat and went away.

Jeremiah 2:13
My people have committed two sins:
They have forsaken me,
The spring of living water
And dug their own cisterns,
Broken cisterns that cannot hold water.

Chapter 5

Why are you angry?

Now Abel kept flocks but Cain worked the soil. In the course of time Cain brought some of the fruits of the soil as an offering to the Lord. But Abel brought fat portions from some of the firstborn of his flock. The Lord looked with favor on Abel and his offering, but on Cain and his offering he did not look with favor. So Cain was very angry and his face was downcast.

Then the Lord said to Cain, "Why are you angry?"

Genesis 4:2-6a

The effects of the good and evil fruit took a treacherous turn in Adam and Eve's son Cain. We don't know much about their children until they made an offering to God of the fruit of their labor. Cain, a farmer, offered fruit from the soil. Abel, a herder, offered fat portions from his flock. God favored Abel's gift; the story does not explain why, although the writer of Hebrews suggests that Abel offered his gift in faith and Cain did not (*Hebrews 11:4*). At any rate, Cain was seething. He might have been thinking that this whole gift business had been his bright idea. And it was a very religious idea! Why wasn't he getting credit? *Who does Abel think he is anyway? How dare my gift be rejected!*

God sought him out and asked why he was angry. He did not tell him that anger was a sin or that he shouldn't be angry. It was an invitation to pour out his heart. Cain could have told God what was making him so mad: perhaps envy of his little brother, how easy things seemed to come to him, or his own fear that he would always come up short. He could have told God about the motives in his heart that might have spoiled the gift he had offered. Maybe Cain had been living with this anger for so long, nursing it, keeping count of all the wrongs he could remember, all the "bad" things Abel had done to him, all the ways Abel had outshone him, that he had lost all affection for him, and now he was dominated by anger toward his brother.

Getting to the bottom of our anger is really important to God. (We'll see him address this issue more than once). If Cain could stop being offended for five minutes, he might encounter something crucial. Beneath the anger, the jealousy, the thoughts of retaliation, Cain might find that his rage had little to do with Abel and everything to do with his own shadow self, or that he was in truth afraid not only was his gift unacceptable, but maybe he was not acceptable, not loveable. These notions can fuel anger, anxiety, envy, and rivalry.

If Cain could put aside his anger, he might be able to look at who he had become. He might not like what he sees—but he could then choose to change. If he could only suspend the anger for a little bit, he might see that in spite of his rejected gift, God was not rejecting him. If Cain could be honest about his fears and his sadness, and his own dark heart, he might then see God standing in front of him—seeking *Cain* out, not Abel. He might see the concern and love of a father. He might be so happy to know that God loved him too, that he had a second chance, he could forget all about his brother and his own botched gift to God. He might hear God when he said, "If you do what is right, will you not be accepted?" (*Genesis 4:7*). He too could make an acceptable gift. It was not too late. God would accept his gift if offered from the right heart. In his gratitude, he could then offer that gift.

If anger is rooted in an old wound, real or imagined, it can take on a long life of its own. It can be a veil through which we see everything. We read our own angry thoughts into everyone we run into, or everyone who reminds us of our "brother." Anger can become so intolerable in us that sometimes we learn how to trigger it in those around us and have them do all the ranting. Anger also gets expressed as resentment. We don't say anything, but rather judge and criticize in our heart. If we judge our "brother" in our heart, chances are he knows it whether we

38 - PAULA PATTON QUINN

say anything or not. When anger takes root, we can't really see the person we're mad at. If it becomes a lifestyle, we can't see anything clearly. It robs us of what we want most in life—love, laughter, friendship and belonging. Unless of course what we want even more is to be right.

Anger begets more anger and it can fuel and be fueled by revenge, which is exactly where Cain was headed, regardless of the consequences. It is so very hard to repent, to just let the anger go, to change our thoughts and feelings, but I know a person can change. I've seen it happen.

My father had a huge heart, a great capacity to love, and a terrible temper. When he was sixty-five, he had a serious heart attack. After he recovered, the doctor told him he had to get rid of stress. From that time forward, he never lost his temper again, and he lived to be ninety. Not only did he not lose his temper, he never even appeared to be angry. He just stopped— for twenty-five years!

There's a backstory. My grandfather—my father's father— had a terrible temper, too. He was so mean that my father hated him. After my daddy's heart attack, he had an interesting conversation with his oldest sister about their father. My grandfather had been sick almost from the time my daddy was born and died when he was only twelve. His sister was quite a bit older and had known their father long before he got sick.

So my father asked his sister if their father had always been mean. My aunt said, on the contrary, before he got sick he had been a kind and sweet man, but his illness triggered or unleashed a frightening temper.

After this conversation and for the first time in his life, my daddy put a picture of his father on the bedroom wall. No therapy, no priest, just an admonition from a doctor about stress and a conversation with his sister about the dad he never really knew. And he was off the anger merry-go-round.

Pause. Take a breath. Who are you mad at and what makes you angry? What grudges are you nursing? If you take off the anger (like removing a mask), what face is there? Who would you be without the anger? Imagine how it would feel if you just quit being mad. To stop living on a merry-go-round of anger (or self pity or fear to name a few more merry-go-rounds), you have to get off, even if no one follows you, even if the apology you're convince is owed is never forthcoming. It can be scary. Sometimes you even have to jump while the merry-go-round is still turning, even if your sparring partner remains stuck in his own dance of anger (and is going to assume that he's finally "won").

It's not enough to pretend you are not angry, or to quit acting mean. You need to change on the inside. God offered Cain a listening ear, a safe place to vent. He tried to interrupt the anger. His question—"Why are you angry?"—was a call for reflection and an invitation to real change.

It's an opportunity for us too, to allow the healer to set us free. It's God-sponsored therapy.

Prayer

Father,

Why am I angry? The first thing that comes to mind in response to your question is that I get mad at members of my family when they are not being who I want them to be.

The second thing is that I get angry at members of my own family when they criticize me for not being who they want me to be.

The third thing is when my agenda is interrupted. I get angry after I say "Yes" when I want to say "No," and I blame the person who put me in that position to begin with. I get mad at my spouse when I am unhappy because surely it is somehow his fault. The list goes on and on.

Lord, could you, would you, please disassemble this web? Call to my mind, in the moment, that I have another choice. Give me the great gift of humility. I will let you sort out who is right or wrong. Help me to quit being the judge, even of myself.

Amen

Please take an opportunity now to be still before the Lord. Then in a journal or notebook, write down your thoughts as you meditate on the question "Why are you angry?" Maybe later read the questions in "Further Reflections" and the scripture in "Lectio Divina" and journal your thoughts.

Spend a few minutes in quiet contemplation. Listen for the Holy Spirit and speak from your heart to God. Take a few minutes to listen or share the silence in the presence of God.

Why are you angry?

Further Reflections

1. How do you use anger to control the people around you?

2. Some say the root of anger is fear. Do you see a connection between something you fear and something or someone that makes you angry?

Lectio Divina

Ephesians 4:26-27 and 31-32

In your anger, do not sin. Do not let the sun go down while you are still angry, and do not give the devil a foothold. Get rid of all bitterness, rage and anger, brawling and slander, along with every form of malice. Be kind and compassionate to one another, forgiving each other, just as in Christ, God forgave you.

I John 2:9-11

Anyone who claims to be in the light but hates his brother is still in the darkness. Whoever loves his brother lives in the light, and there is nothing in him to make him stumble. But whoever hates his brother is in the darkness and walks around in the darkness; he does not know where he is going, because the darkness has blinded him.

Chapter 6

Why is your face downcast?

Then the Lord said to Cain, "Why is your face downcast?
If you do what is right will you not be accepted? But if you do
not do what is right, sin is crouching at the door; it desires to
have you, but you must master it."

Genesis 4:6-7

God continued questioning Cain, asking not only why he was angry, but also why he was downcast. The questions came in quick succession, but perhaps there was a long pause between each while God waited for Cain to respond. He didn't.

Because Cain's gift was not acceptable, he may have felt like a failure; his feelings were hurt. God did not chide Cain for feeling downcast or suggest that this emotion was unacceptable, but he did try to address it. In the same way anger does, sadness or depression can intensify, persist, and ensnare us. If being downcast becomes intolerable and we are motivated to get rid of it, we can find ourselves doing things we might regret later. Our tender hearts make us vulnerable and sometimes that feels like weakness. After awhile the feelings take their toll, we just want them to end, and if we blame someone else, our solution can be to retaliate against them. If we blame ourselves, we can retaliate against ourselves.

Cain wrestled with both anger and hopelessness. When those feelings form a partnership, the results can be lethal. Cain was already thinking, "What better way out of anger and being downcast than to get rid of the one who is causing all this?" Given what happens next, it seems Cain would rather feel right and take revenge on Abel than deal with his feelings and answer God's questions. He believed revenge would make him feel better and end his downcast state.

Anger might feel like a welcome relief to depression. Anger energizes while depression immobilizes. We often cling to one to diminish the other. We often feel like we haven't the power to let go of either one.

God's words to Cain suggested that Cain had a choice. Despite how overwhelming his emotions were, by inviting Cain to talk about them, God opened a way out of their grip. There was still time. The very act of talking with God about his downcast soul would allow some space and light on the inside of Cain. He could assess his unacceptable gift with honesty. He could take a look at his relationship with Abel. He could look at his emotions to discover if this could lessen their intensity. He could hear God's perspective. He could make fresh choices instead of being driven to act out his raw emotions.

God ended the dialogue by giving Cain a warning. "If you do what is right, will you not be accepted? But if you do not do what is right, sin is crouching at your door; it desires to have you, but you must master it" (*Genesis 4:7*). We can see a correlation between doing the right thing and overcoming the anger and depression as well as a correlation between Cain's anger and depression and the sin that was crouching at the door. The implication was that turning away from anger and depression would also spell the defeat of the sin lying in wait. This particular "crouching tiger" wanted to dominate Cain. According to God, sin "wanted" him. Also according to God, he could master it.

I so wish Cain had looked at God right at this point and said, "But how? How do I do what you're telling me? It doesn't *feel* like I have a choice." I wish Cain had asked because I would so like to know God's answer, God's counsel, his secret to getting rid of depression. At this stage Cain could still choose somehow to do just that, but he was in peril of losing that freedom, of being in bondage to something that would ultimately dominate him. Cain barely engaged with God.

This choice was not just for Cain. Before him, it was the choice for Adam and Eve as well. They could have chosen the tree that brought life instead of the tree that brought death. It becomes the fork in the road for the nation of Israel that is to come. It's the choice before us all, over and over again. God made an appeal to Cain to exercise his will. He could choose: life or death. Many of us know someone who is losing or has lost this battle: someone whose knee jerk response is to get mad, someone whose "normal" is depression, someone who uses resentment and disappointment to justify lashing out or quitting or using that drug one more time.

We can be the one who allows envy to feed self-pity, who poisons all our relationships with a sense of entitlement, the one who focuses on all the reasons to be sad instead of all the reasons to be happy or grateful, the one who replaces a sense of inadequacy with contempt. Maybe the first step away from the crouching predator who seeks to master us is to give God our attention, to listen to his questions and respond from the heart, to tell him why we are downcast. At least that is what this passage suggests.

There's one more aspect of this conversation. God cautioned Cain about the sin that would come to dominate him if he gave into it, but he didn't warn him about what *he* would do; God did not try to bully Cain with threats into doing the right thing. The freedom God gave Cain—and gives us as well—is breathtaking.

Centuries later Jesus told a story about two brothers (*Luke 15*). Both brothers were downcast and/or angry, each for his own reasons. Their lives played out in very different ways. The older brother was a dutiful son, the younger a scoundrel. The younger son returned home, after having squandered all the money his father had given him on wild living. He was beaten down, remorseful, full of shame, and hungry. When he arrived home, he discovered something amazing about his father, something he would never have guessed. His father wasn't mad at him. He wasn't ashamed of him. He had never given up on him. He'd been on the lookout for him. His father ran to greet him when he saw this son finally trudging home. He kissed his son's dirty face. He made a big deal about *him*, the ne'er do well! He threw him an extravagant party, the kind fit for a conquering hero. The young man at last saw the heart of his own father and knew he really loved him. In fact, he was loved to an extravagant degree. That love was his birthright, but he had never before perceived it.

The older brother could not tolerate his father's generosity. He refused to join the party. Hadn't his brother shamed the family? And hadn't he himself done everything right? Where was his barbeque? He was furious. He was so resentful that he missed the heart of his father. If his father had treasured duty and hard work above all, then he had been on the right track.

His father didn't love him because he was so good. His father knew his obedience was tainted by his pride and resentment. He loved him anyway. He reminded him that everything he had was his. The love his father had for him, even as he pleaded for him to come inside and join the family celebration, did not seem to break through the barrier of his anger and downcast spirit.

Jesus made a point in this parable that he doesn't want us to miss, no matter what part we play in the story: our heavenly father has a heart of love for us.

How children see their fathers, how we see God, who we think he is, makes all the difference. How we see ourselves is irrevocably tied to this, too. All the insecurity about how we measure up, how we compare, all the focus on getting ahead, and our dispirited, downcast moods, can sabotage us, leaving us vulnerable to their mastery over us. We have planks in our eyes, even when God pleads with us to come into his banquet.

God asked Cain to choose another way. What if Cain had looked in God's eyes and seen his compassion? What if he had seen that it was not a competition? What if he too had seen the Father's extravagant love? The scary part is that even God himself could not convince Cain to make the right choice.

What have your sadness, anger, and jealousy cost you? What lingering hurt has a grip on your life? Despair can set in and cloud our vision. We miss the new path that God encourages us to take. In your own time of being downcast, listen for your heavenly father. He may ask you to tell him all about it.

Prayer

Father,

Thank you so much that you ask these questions. You invite us to pour out our hearts to you, to come clean. Thank you also that you warn us. Thank you that you let the consequences of our very mistaken choices lead us back to you and your river of grace. Thank you for all the lessons that teach humility. Thank you that you trust us with such freedom. Thank you that you can deliver us from our own foolhardy choices, that you keep offering redemption.

Please make me strong and good.

Amen

Please take an opportunity now to be still before the Lord. Then in a journal or notebook, write down your thoughts as you meditate on the question "Why is your face downcast?" Maybe later read the questions in "Further Reflections" and the scripture in "Lectio Divina" and journal your thoughts.

Spend a few minutes in quiet contemplation. Listen for the Holy Spirit and speak from your heart to God. Take a few minutes to listen or share the silence in the presence of God.

Why is your face downcast?

Further Reflections

1. If you're feeling downcast now, or even if you're not, remember a time when you were, and write a letter to God telling all the reasons why.

2. Have you felt the persistent love of your own father? What has been the impact of that on your life? Your understanding about God?

Lectio Divina

Psalm 42:11

Why are you downcast, O my soul? Why so disturbed within me? Put your hope in God, for I will yet praise him, my Savior and my God.

Luke 15:28-31

"The older brother became angry and refused to go in. So his father went out and pleaded with him. But he answered his father, 'Look! All these years I've been slaving for you and never disobeyed your orders. Yet you never gave me even a young goat so I could celebrate with my friends. But when this son of yours, who has squandered your property with prostitutes, comes home, you kill the fattened calf for him!' 'My son,' the father said, 'you are always with me, and everything I have is yours.'"

Chapter 7

Then the Lord said to Cain, "Where is your brother Abel?"

Now Cain said to his brother Abel, "Let's go out to the field." And while they were in the field, Cain attacked his brother Abel and killed him.

Then the Lord said to Cain, "Where is your brother Abel?"

"I don't know," he replied. "Am I my brother's keeper?"

Genesis 4: 8-9

Like a lamb led to the slaughter, Cain invited Abel to a lonely field to kill him. Anyone would call it premeditated murder. We don't know how much time elapsed between the crime and his encounter with God. The adrenaline could have still been running high, or maybe enough time had passed that Cain thought he'd gotten away with it. His parents, wondering where Abel had wandered off, had probably already asked Cain, "Where is your brother?" I can imagine them feeling anxious, calling out for their missing son, asking Cain for any information. God, however, already knew the answer. Abel's body lay in that field. His death was so horrific that even the earth cried out (*Genesis 4:10*).

"Where is your brother?" could have been God's summons to Cain to confess the truth and unburden himself of his terrible guilt. It could have been an attempt to prick Cain's conscience and elicit some genuine remorse. He could have been giving Cain a final opportunity to tell the truth. The question harkens back to the first thing God said when he came looking for Adam and Eve in the garden: "Where are you?"

God not only asks us where we are, but where our brother is as well. The question implies that God sees us in community and wants us to see that, too. It also implies that we have to give an accounting to God himself.

Perhaps the question reminded Cain of the way it used to be, when he and his kid brother were inseparable buddies, built forts together, shot hoops, and climbed trees. No doubt Eve had put Cain in charge of his little brother many times. Maybe Cain resented it, had always begrudged this younger intruder.

Maybe he was afraid his brother would forever outshine him. The favored gift was just the final straw. Will Cain let the tragedy and the terrible consequences of his unbridled anger and betrayal seep into his heart, or will he plant his feet further in the camp of the enemy—the sin crouching at the door?

If he let down his guard for a minute, he might realize what he had done. The terrible reality and finality might knock him off his feet. Cain himself might cry out, "What have I done?" He might let grief for his brother's death, even at his own hands, replace his awful pride. He might see the tragedy he had wrought and thereby set about his transformation, his reformation. In order to be saved, Cain must first recognize the truth of the situation: his ghastly transgression, his own vengeance, his pride and self-righteousness, the pain he has caused his family, and the harm that cannot be repaired.

Instead he lied: "I don't know," and then, chin sticking out, said, "Am I my brother's keeper?" The implied answer, the truth that Cain doesn't want to be true, is, "Yes, you are his keeper. We are all each other's keepers."

God had already warned Cain. The warning itself indicated what God wanted: for Cain to rise up and fight the sin crouching at the door. God had been willing to give him a do-over on the unacceptable offering. God had rooted for Cain to overcome his demon. Now that we know Cain better, we can see why his gift had been unacceptable. The anger and pride that spilled over into murder lurked within even as he made his original offering.

Cain and Abel's offerings to God raise questions about our own offerings and our sacrifices of time and money, whether they are offered to God, to friends and family, or to charity. Our gifts can be tainted by our pride or anger or false religiosity. Resentment can accompany our gifts. Sometimes our gifts are just dregs, or we give because we secretly expect a reward—applause and recognition at least—or worse, a pay-off or a bought favor. Our gifts can be like bribes. Cain was the one who suggested the idea of offering a gift to God. Maybe it was to appease. Maybe he had already done something wrong but instead of coming clean, changing or repenting, he took a short cut and made an offering instead. Did he see God as a judge to be placated while Abel saw him as a father to be thanked?

This question expresses one of God's major concerns. Our intimate relationships and the love we demonstrate for our brothers and sisters is of utmost importance to God. We would rather make an offering to God or charity, check it off our to-do list, and walk away feeling righteous. Then God says, "Where is your brother?"

Hear God ask: "Where are you? What have you done? Why are you angry? Why are you depressed? Where is your brother?" We need to see the authority behind them and the wisdom and love inherent in them. The questions sound simple, but the answers can lead to an abundant life, or a soulless life, or even to death.

Prayer

Father,

There are plenty of people in this world who are "ahead" of me: more spiritual, more beautiful, more successful, more intelligent, more friends, more confidence, and more money. It looks like life is easy for them. Lord, here and now I ask your blessing on them.

Also sometimes I look at others and feel superior. Please forgive me. Cause me to see whom I have hurt, ignored, or expelled due to my own arrogance, selfishness, anger, or jealousy.

I have also experienced being part of a community, both of family and friends, and just to play my part, even when it's a small part, can be such a pleasure. Thank you for my own brother, my family, and my friends.

Amen

Please take an opportunity now to be still before the Lord. Then in a journal or notebook, write down your thoughts as you meditate on the question "What have you done?" Maybe later read the questions in "Further Reflections" and the scripture in "Lectio Divina" and journal your thoughts.

Spend a few minutes in quiet contemplation. Listen for the Holy Spirit and speak from your heart to God. Take a few minutes to listen or share the silence in the presence of God.

Where is your brother (your sister, your friend)?

Further Reflections

1. Who might God be pointing out as your brother or sister that you might want to ignore or expel from your life?

2. Can you imagine a reconciliation or a first step in that direction? Are you willing to pray every day for a month for them to be blessed?

Lectio Divina

Psalm 51:16-17 (The Passion Translation)
For the source of your pleasure is not in my performance or the sacrifices I might offer to you.

The fountain of your pleasure is found in the sacrifice of my shattered heart before you.

You will not despise my tenderness as I humbly bow down at your feet.

Luke 10:29
But he wanted to justify himself, so he asked Jesus, "and who is my neighbor?"

I John 3:12
We should not be like Cain, who yielded to the Evil One and brutally murdered his own brother, Abel. And why did he murder him? Because his own actions were evil and his brother's righteous.

Chapter 8

What have you done?

Then the Lord said, "What have you done? Listen! Your brother's blood cries out to me from the ground."

Genesis 4:10

"What have you done?" This is the identical question God asked Adam and Eve in the garden. Then it seemed like a lament. Now it sounds like wrath. Unlike his parents, Cain didn't attempt an answer. He either felt no horror at his actions, could not face what he had done, or was still justifying the whole thing in his mind. He maintained his defiance before God. But God grasped the horror, the finality, and the terrible consequences to follow. Cain would have to be banished. He could not be trusted to wreak any more havoc on this family.

This time God didn't ask Cain why. The time for exploring the heart's motivations was over. God already knew Cain hated his brother and blamed him, and he could see Cain felt no remorse and he would go on hating and blaming. By now Cain's heart had hardened. Adam and Eve's bickering blame had turned very ugly in their first born. It was time to pronounce what was to come. Abel's blood cried out. The ground had already been cursed; now Cain was cursed. "Now you are under a curse and driven from the ground, which opened its mouth to receive your brother's blood from your hand. When you work the ground, it will no longer yield its crops for you. You will be a restless wanderer on the earth" (*Genesis 4:11-12*).

Cain's job had been tilling the soil, working the ground to produce food. He had offered this produce to God. When he killed his brother, it was possibly in the same field where he tilled and worked. But no more. He was exiled from home and his livelihood. Two main sources of human identity were lost in the aftermath of fratricide. He was sentenced to be a vagabond for the rest of his life. Even if he tried to settle down, he would never be at home again.

Cain couldn't believe his punishment: "My punishment is more than I can bear… you are driving me from the land, and I will be hidden from your presence." (*Genesis 4:13-14*). Where did he get that idea that he was "hidden from the presence" of God? God did not tell Cain he was withdrawing his presence; Cain jumped to that conclusion.

Cain must have known something of the presence. He at least believed it offered protection. Maybe he had known the comfort of the presence of God, and the guidance as well. Cain took these gifts for granted and treasured them too late, and now he was convinced his expulsion would include the absence of God. Without his family, and believing he was isolated from the very presence of God, too late he saw that he will be extremely vulnerable, "…whoever finds me now will kill me." (*Genesis 4:14*).

We expect the next line to be, "These are the consequences," or "You reap what you sow." Isn't it about time for God to initiate an eye for an eye? God doesn't respond with anything like that. Instead he said, "Not so, if anyone kills Cain, he will suffer vengeance seven times over" (*Genesis 4:15*).

How amazing that God promised Cain protection in his travels. God put a mark, a protective emblem on him, so that even in exile, no one would harm him. He had taken his brother's life, yet God promised to guard him for as long as he lived. This is mind-boggling. It is the grace of God and the justice of God.

I wonder if the indelible mark God placed on Cain would remind him that, even alone, he was still and would always be protected by God. In some sense he was still in his presence. In fact he would never wander beyond the range of this God.

Perhaps you know someone who paid or is still paying a high price for a terrible act of jealous rage. Maybe they are filled with regrets and remorse, or still blame the downward spiral of their lives on somebody else. Maybe it's you. Maybe you've become a castaway, cut off from your family, your friends, or your career. Even if you can't go home again or it's too late to make amends, consider God's faithful promise to protect Cain for the rest of his life. Can you believe, in spite of what you may have done, God is still somehow with you?

This episode of Cain and Abel and the sequence of questions God posed can instruct us. We don't have to let anger and depression dominate us. However, if we refuse to change, if we refuse to engage with God, we are in dangerous territory. The twin demons, anger and depression, can master us and rob us of our freedom to choose a different path. They can isolate us from our family. They leave us not only ungrounded, but unable to put down roots. They blind us to the truth and love of God. They rob us of his felt presence. In the end they enforce their own kind of banishment.

Prayer

Father,

I have tasted your presence. It is sheer gift. It is treasure. In all truth, sometimes I have amnesia about it and go for days forgetting what I know or who I really am, also forgetting your generosity and grace.

There are so many things I ask you for, but I'm telling you that no matter what, no matter if there is no food in the fridge, no promise of a harvest, no assets in the bank, no matter what I don't have, what I need and want most is your presence.

You are my treasure.

Amen

Please take an opportunity now to be still before the Lord. Then in a journal or notebook, write down your thoughts as you meditate on the question "What have you done?" Maybe later read the questions in "Further Reflections" and the scripture in "Lectio Divina" and journal your thoughts.

Spend a few minutes in quiet contemplation. Listen for the Holy Spirit and speak from your heart to God. Take a few minutes to listen or share the silence in the presence of God.

What have you done?

Further Reflections

1. What have you done that you most regret? What has been done to you that was the most difficult to deal with?

2. Take some time now and ask God to come alongside you. Ask him to make you sensitive to his presence. Persist.

Lectio Divina

Exodus 33:14-15

The Lord replied, "My Presence will go with you, and I will give you rest."

Then Moses said to Him, "If your Presence does not go with us, do not send us up from here."

Revelation 3:20

Here I am! I stand at the door and knock. If anyone hears my voice and opens the door, I will come in and eat with him, and he with me.

PART 2

ORIGIN OF ISRAEL

Chapters 9 - 13

After Adam and Eve, after Cain and Abel, and later Noah and the flood, God initiated a new plan to win his people back to his heart and his ways. He chose a man named Abram and his wife Sarai (later to be changed to Abraham and Sarah), to birth a new family—a blessed family. Adam and Eve lost their home, and their beautiful garden because they listened to the serpent and his temptation to eat the deadly fruit. Now God offered a fresh start to Abraham and Sarah, an opportunity to listen to him (again), follow his instructions, and inherit a new homeland.

Will they believe God, trust God, and do what he says? There is a close connection between believing and doing. Will they leave their birthplace and journey to a new land—a place God promised will be their very own forever? God has not forgotten our deep longing for a home, a place of belonging, a place of peace. They go.

God continued his very intimate, personal encounters with the people who came to be honored as the patriarchs and matri-archs of God's special people, as well as with some who would be considered quite ordinary. We see these men and women in very human circumstances. For Abraham and Sarah, faith in God must have felt like a risky endeavor. They had to give up one home and travel into unknown territory, all on the word of an unseen God. They waver between great trust in him and severe doubt. In fact, they seem always to be taking two steps forward and one step back; we are so much like them.

The great time and effort God took to engage with them, to ask them questions, and to indulge their questions encourages us. We are heartened, even transformed, to see what great things happen when someone a lot like us believes God.

Many of these stories involve God making or reiterating promises. In the context of these stories, God makes unilateral promises to Abraham and Sarah. He promises them land, a son, and ultimately a descendant who will one day bless all people. Some of us follow or expect the fulfillment of a promise, too, maybe even a promise from God.

Before you begin, take a few minutes and meditate on "promise."

Chapter 9

Hagar, servant of Sarai, where have you come from, and where are you going?

Now Sarai, Abram's wife, had borne him no children. But she had an Egyptian maidservant named Hagar; so she said to Abram, "The Lord has kept me from having children. Go sleep with my maidservant; perhaps I can build a family through her."

Abram agreed to what Sarai said. So after Abram had been living in Canaan ten years, Sarai his wife took her Egyptian maidservant Hagar and gave her to her husband to be his wife. He slept with Hagar and she conceived.

When she knew she was pregnant, she began to despise her mistress. Then Sarai said to Abram, "You are responsible for the wrong I am suffering. I put my servant in your arms, and now that she knows she is pregnant, she despises me. May the Lord judge between you and me."

"Your servant is in your hands," Abram said. "Do with her whatever you think best." Then Sarai mistreated Hagar; so she fled from her.

The angel of the Lord found Hagar near a spring in the desert… And he said to her, "Hagar, servant of Sarai, where have you come from and where are you going?"

Genesis 16:1-8

God promised Abraham and Sarah land, but he made another promise as well. He guaranteed the childless couple a very special child, and not only one child, but a whole tribe, a nation and multiple descendants from the one child to follow. The final promise was one "offspring" through whom "all nations on earth will be blessed" (*Genesis 22:18*). Abraham and Sarah awaited the birth with great eagerness. Time passed. Nothing happened.

Then Sarah got a bright idea; she would "help" God. "Given human history," she might have said to herself, "God needs all the help he can get." Plus, "Given how long this is taking, maybe this is what he meant us to do all along." Sarah lent her servant Hagar to Abraham for a tryst and Abraham obliged.

As this part of the story opens, Hagar was indeed pregnant with Abraham's child, and she flaunted it. The "nobody" slave had become a "somebody."

I picture her as a teenager, sold to Abraham and Sarah, separated from her family, at last with a little cachet because she carried the child of this man of means.

Sarah had never known such jealousy. This other woman was carrying the child promised to her! It doesn't seem to matter that this was her idea. She became so angry that she hit Hagar (according to some translations).

Hagar then ran into the desert when, all of a sudden, in the midst of her fear and despair, God showed up. The Lord said to her, "Where have you come from and where are you going?"

Hagar answered only the first part of this question. "I'm

running from my mistress," adding no embellishment to the story.

Then the Lord made Hagar an amazing promise. Sarah and Abraham weren't the only ones who would have descendants too numerous to count. She would, too. God had room in his heart for this lowly woman—this servant who was used and abused and now lording her pregnancy over Sarah. She was not disqualified from receiving a blessing as well.

God instructed Hagar to name her son "Ishmael" which means "God hears." He has, after all, done exactly that. He also told her Ishmael would be a difficult child, but she will receive a daily reminder in her first born of this momentous day: the day God sought her out, called her by her name, and gave her the instructions and the courage to go back. She would always remember that God heard her.

Maybe, like Hagar, we wrestle inside ourselves, feeling like nobodies, trying to be somebodies. The truth is we are both. We, like Hagar, are ordinary, a mix of good and bad. Maybe we also were induced or forced to do something unfortunate, something with scary, unforeseen consequences.

God also knows and loves us. We are blessed and gifted beyond measure, and very special. Believing only in our ordinariness and knowing how much we have already contributed to the messes in our lives, it is hard to believe God has greatness in mind for us, much less that we possess special gifts already bestowed or that he wants to give us even more.

It's even harder to believe he has already planted his likeness in each of us or he wants to bless us at all. Deep down we know we don't deserve his kindness, so maybe his blessings are not about what we deserve.

Hagar came from servitude. She was powerless. Maybe she believed she was worth only crumbs, but that is not the way God saw her. By asking her the questions, "Where have you come from and where are you going?" he conferred on her great dignity. He was interested in her and in what she had to say about her life. He esteemed her. Not only did she have a destiny, she had some control over it, despite her circumstances.

The first part of God's question—"Where have you come from?"—invites you to look back. What events have led you to this point in your life? If you are old enough, the answer might be long and complicated; if you are very young, then you might not have much to say. Here are some things to consider: where you grew up, your family, your roots, and your more recent experiences.

The second part—"Where are you going?"—is equally important. First, consider if you even know where you are going. Do you sense momentum in your life or are you stuck? If you have dreams, goals, and a destination in mind, consider your preparation and resources. Consider if you are sabotaging your heart's desire by supplying reasons why it won't or can't happen, or if you might be doing things that are counter-productive.

Hagar did not respond to this second question. She either had no answer or she didn't want to divulge what she thought or planned. Since it is God who asked, it is an important question worth our consideration. Hagar appeared to be on the run with no particular endpoint except "away."

Maybe you have run from a bad situation. Did you have an end in mind or an idea of what you would count as a good destination? Perhaps you are drifting and hoping to get somewhere merely "nice," merely okay. Maybe you are so caught up with making it through the day that you have given up on grand goals. Maybe you have finally achieved your goal but found its promise hollow. Maybe it's hard to believe God still has a destiny for you.

Your response to this question is not to figure out what God wants to hear. God just asks you to share your heart and your thoughts. This intimacy can be deeply transforming by itself, but pay close attention because he might share his vision for your life.

If you are lost and need directions—listen. If you are hopeless and need hope—listen. If you are trapped and you need a way out or a way through—listen. Let Hagar be your model. Believe God hears you, he calls you by name, sees you in your wilderness, can speak to you of your destiny, and can give you specific instructions.

God convinced Hager to return. She knew everyone would still see her as Sarah's servant, but she also realized how special she truly was—that the God of the universe knew her name, paid her a visit, and spoke a prophecy over her. Her circumstances won't define her anymore; her private encounter with God changed everything.

Every once in awhile, God asks questions that invite a reflection on life: What led you to this place? Where are you headed? These questions are "taking stock" kind of questions. They suggest that life is a journey and often it's necessary to get your bearings, to check the map, and decipher where you are on the journey. What have you lived through? Are you on a good path now? At a crossroads? Making one more trip around the mountain only to arrive at the same old place?

Whether you are just starting out or closing in on the end of a season of your life, these personal conversations with God give meaning, restore confidence, and make life fun. Meditating on the questions in the presence of God—seeking him—just might jump start a conversation with him that can change everything.

Prayer

Lord,

When I look back at my life, I know I was fortunate. I had a happy, safe, and secure childhood. That is a huge blessing and I am so grateful. I've been blessed as an adult, too, but the road has not always been easy.

Frankly by now I thought I would be coasting, but life is still challenging and still unfolding in unexpected ways. I so wish I could talk all this over with my mother because I would love to know how she faced this part of her journey.

Before I can even begin to take stock, I ask you to make me aware of your presence. Come Holy Spirit and settle me down.

Please show me the patterns of my life and the events that are significant in your eyes. Show me the meaning of my present circumstances. Who do you want me to be now? Who do you want to be for me now? Show me your vision of the person you created me to be, what you created me to accomplish now, at this particular time. Please infuse me with the zest and energy to follow you every day of the journey.

Amen

Settle down in the presence of the Lord and meditate on this question, "Where have you come from and where are you going?" Reflect about whatever comes to mind. Take time later to contemplate the questions in Further Reflections and the Bible verses below. Remember the stages of lectio divina: read, meditate, pray and contemplate.

Where have you come from and where are you going?

Further Reflections

1. Make a timeline of your life and mark it with what you believe are the most significant moments, the turning points, of your life.

2. Share your timeline with God and ask if he has any additions or corrections.

3. Ask him what's next. Listen. Then write down any thoughts that come to mind.

Lectio Divina

Jeremiah 6:16
This is what the Lord says:
"Stand at the crossroads and look;
ask for the ancient paths,
ask where the good way is, and walk in it,
and you will find rest for your souls."

Isaiah 30:21
Whether you turn to the right or to the left, your ears will hear a voice behind you, saying, "This is the way; walk in it."

Chapter 10

Why did Sarah laugh and say, "Will I really have a child, now that I am old?"

Then the Lord said, "I will surely return to you about this time next year, and Sarah your wife will have a son."

Now Sarah was listening at the entrance to the tent, which was behind him. Abraham and Sarah were already old and well advanced in years, and Sarah was past the age of childbearing.

So Sarah laughed to herself as she thought, "After I am worn out and my master is old, will I now have this pleasure?"

Then the Lord said to Abraham, "Why did Sarah laugh and say, 'Will I really have a child, now that I am old?'"

Genesis 3:10-11a

It is heartbreaking to want a child and not be able to conceive. Then someone tells you, maybe a fertility specialist, that indeed you will be able to have a baby. You buy a crib and decorate the nursery. You collect onesies and stock up on diapers. You wait.

Sarah was an old woman by the time the Lord showed up out of the blue and reiterated the old promise. She had folded up the baby clothes and put them away long ago. She had gotten on with her life, she had buried the promise that she would have a child.

As the story opened, Sarah was busy with preparations for the surprise visitors (the angel of the Lord plus two more angels). She was in her tent while Abraham entertained them. One of the angels asked where Sarah was. She was in her tent, but she was also eavesdropping on the party.

The Lord God (or his angel) repeated the very old promise he first made to Abraham when he and his wife were closer to childbearing age: the promised son would be born, and in one year's time. Sarah laughed. The scripture says that she laughed to herself, and I picture her leaning against the stove, perhaps with a dishtowel pressed to her mouth to muffle the noise.

Why did she laugh? Because the very idea was preposterous. She was old; Abraham was old. She was well past the point of faith, hope, or even longing for the prophecy to come true. Perhaps she had even resigned herself to Ishmael as heir apparent.

I love that she laughed. She's a hero of the faith, the great matriarch, but she possessed almost zero faith when the Lord said, "one more year." She might have thought this was nonsense, or it's better to laugh than to have a little hope, only to be disappointed again. Or maybe a very small window was cracked open in her heart of hearts—a little light, a little fresh air—and after all this waiting, maybe she dared to hope again.

Why did God ask this question? Maybe he was suggesting that, as outlandish as it was to expect that Sarah could now give birth, it was even more extraordinary to doubt that God would fulfill his promise.

Sarah was not the first to laugh. A few years before, when Abraham was 99, God held a private conversation with him. The Lord repeated to Abraham the promise of a son to come from Sarah. Abraham laughed so hard he fell to the ground. So God repeated, "...your wife Sarah will have a son, and you will call him Isaac." Significantly, the name "Isaac" means "he laughs." Maybe God laughed, too! Both Abraham and Sarah were astonished to think the promise of long ago might come true.

Put yourself in Sarah's shoes. Is there a dream you've had, a long hoped-for desire, even a prophetic word spoken to you, which now seems impossible? Do you think you are too old for this dream? Perhaps you believe you have done too much damage along your life's path for the promise to be resurrected. Maybe you have buried your heart's desires because you believe they will never be fulfilled, or God made a promise to you that has just taken too long to come true. You suspect God changed his mind, or you got it all wrong, or you've done something that has made you ineligible.

God makes promises that aren't fulfilled for a long time. You might think if he gave you (like he gave Abraham and Sarah) a specified date, say one year's time, it would be easier to believe, to have faith. I'm not so sure. Sometimes God tells us something and, like Adam and Eve, a serpent snatches the word away before we even begin to believe. The standard ploy are the questions, "Did God really say?" or "Was that really God?"

Sometimes before the promise can be fulfilled, painful or difficult things cause us to give up. Or we just get so consumed with our lives that we barely remember the promise. Sometimes it just takes too long. Sometimes we have to contend for the promise. Believing in it and not giving up might be prerequisites for its fulfillment.

Sarah may have laughed in shock or disbelief, but she had not forgotten the promise and neither had God. God spent a lifetime and had multiple encounters with Abraham and Sarah to get them to a place of real faith. After this encounter, Sarah didn't argue with God anymore. You can almost feel her hope rising again. God makes promises and our response is often: "Really?... Could you please confirm... How can I know for sure?" He comes through when all we can offer is a mustard seed of faith.

Reflect for a moment on the contrast between the life of Abraham and Sarah and the life of Adam and Eve. God told Adam and Eve not to eat from the tree of knowledge because it would be the death of them, but they listened to the serpent and ate the fruit anyway. God told Abraham and Sarah to go to a foreign land. He promised them a family.

Abraham and Sarah listened to God and did what he said. This choice of whom to listen to, whom to trust and believe was the turning point for both couples.

It becomes the crossroad for us all. To whom will we listen?

God changed the course of history with these very imperfect people, with people who laughed when God told them his plans.

Prayer

Father,

You know I've been where Sarah is. You have given me a promise and a date certain. I struggled with anxiety and fear. The agitation they stirred up created an overwhelming urge to take the situation into my own hands.

But I held on and I'm so glad I did, not just because I received your promise but because what I was really holding onto was you. When I've lost hope, I don't just want a rescue or even a manifestation, I want deliverance from the tyranny of panic and worry.

Praise be that that is exactly what you want, too.

Amen

Settle down in the presence of the Lord and meditate on this question, "Why did you laugh?" Reflect about whatever comes to mind. Take time later to contemplate the questions in Further Reflections and the Bible verses below. Remember the stages of lectio divina: read, meditate, pray and contemplate.

Why did you laugh?

Further Reflections

1. Have you ever considered that God has a sense of humor? Do you believe he's interested in bringing about joyful circumstances for you? Or in helping you develop a merry heart?

2. Are you inclined to take charge when you feel stuck or trapped or are you more inclined to wait and see what happens? To accept the status quo or make a move?

Lectio Divina

Genesis 21:6
   Sarah said, "God has brought me laughter, and everyone who hears about this will laugh with me."

Psalm 126:2 (The Passion Translation)
   We laughed and laughed and overflowed with gladness. We were left shouting for joy and singing your praise. All the nations saw it and joined in, saying, "The Lord has done great miracles for them!"

Chapter 11

Is anything too hard for the Lord?

Then the Lord said to Abraham, "Why did Sarah laugh and say, 'Will I really have a child, now that I am old?' Is anything too hard for the Lord? I will return to you at the appointed time next year and Sarah will have a son."

Genesis 18:13-14

In the abstract, if anyone asked me, "Is anything too hard for the Lord?" I would reply, that, of course, nothing is too hard for God. But if I had been waiting on the Lord for a while or praying for a long time with no results, I might take my prayer and my expectations off the table. I might assume this situation is too hard for God, even if I never said it out loud. If the situation seemed intractable, or if it required an intervention I couldn't fathom, I might resign myself to the situation and call it acceptance and maturity.

I'm not the only one who has done this. I've heard priests and pastors explain why we really shouldn't expect too much from God. Without realizing it, they diminish him because they're afraid that God won't/can't/never does, or at least is not likely to, answer the prayer of faith. They might add that God quit making promises years ago, that miracles have ceased or were only tall tales to begin with. They want to do two things: 1) protect their people from disappointment, and/or 2) protect God's reputation.

We must settle this question for ourselves, not just once and for all, but every time we come against the highly improbable, if not the impossible. If this God is who he says he is, will he really *do* what he says he will do? Can he really do it?

After God's response to Sarah's laughter, he repeated his promise: "I will return to you at the appointed time next year and Sarah will have a son."

Sarah came out from her tent then, denying what she did. "I did not laugh."

And God said, "Yes, you did laugh." (I see a twinkle in his eye.)

Did God punish her for this?

Did he take the promise and give it to another more faithful woman?

Did he scold her or give her a lecture on faith?

When her laughter, followed by her denial of laughter, subsided, she and Abraham both heard God's question, "Is anything too hard for the Lord?"

Think about what is going on here. God is establishing at the beginning, for this family and for all the families to be born of them, that *nothing it too hard for him*. Nothing! Whether we are deceived and break faith, or are defiant and disobey, or whether we are filled with laughter, even skepticism, instead of meek trust, God wants us to know, to taste and see, that nothing is too hard for him.

Much later God told Abraham to sacrifice Isaac (or, in their lingo, "Laughter"). By that time, Abraham knew nothing was too hard for God, not even bringing his beloved son back from the dead. After a whole lifetime of conversations with God, a lifetime of God keeping his promises, Abraham's trust grew unshakeable. He did exactly what God told him to do, and by this strict obedience he demonstrated radical faith. And God showed Abraham that he, God, was the one to provide the sacrifice. He also established that he had not, nor would he ever, institute child sacrifice as part of this religion.

I have seen the hand of God, sometimes in dramatic ways. I have seen God rescue a child from a hopeless situation; he followed my daughter into the abyss of addiction and brought her out alive and well. This was not too hard for the Lord. God restored my husband from a catastrophic illness. In 2004, he had emergency brain surgery, which triggered liver failure, which then triggered lung failure. God brought him back from the brink of death and into robust health. This was not too hard for the Lord. I have seen God restore a marriage after trust had been broken. I have seen God heal an old man's deeply wounded soul. Not too hard for the Lord.

As I studied this question, I looked up the passage in other translations and discovered quite a different question. Instead of, "Is anything too hard for the Lord?" it read, "Is anything too *wonderful* for the Lord?" (*Young's Literal Translation*).

What a different idea! God was, in effect, saying he knew having her own child was Sarah's dream, a dream she couldn't imagine being fulfilled, but this dream was not too good to be true. *Because nothing is too wonderful for the Lord.* God's promise to Abraham and Sarah and their hearts' desires were at last coming together in their very own baby to be born in one year's time.

People of faith are often trained to believe that God is good in the same sense that bad tasting medicine is good. They are taught to want his will (or to say they do) when they remain secretly afraid of his will. We relegate all sorts of natural disasters to "the will of God." We pray in earnest for something really important and then tack on at the end, "Nevertheless, not my will but thine be done," and in all honesty, many accompany this plea with a sigh or a sense of dread. But here we see that God's will is something wonderful. Abraham and Sarah were challenged to believe that nothing is too wonderful for the Lord. That's the challenge I want.

Sarah laughed at the very promise of God, and Abraham

laughed at the same promise, too. If God were to tell me he was about to do the impossible—and the impossibly wonderful—for me, I might also burst into laughter. But I want to hear God's next words as well, "Is anything too hard or too *wonderful* for me?"

Prayer

Lord,

You have intervened to bring salvation or deliverance or healing or a word of hope to me. I can honestly say that you have brought me or someone I was praying for out of dire circumstances and into wonderful circumstances. You have given me gifts. You have made right and good situations that were dark and hopeless.

I don't doubt that your intentions toward me are good. So why do I still succumb to fear? I still lose sleep in the middle of the night over some fresh problem.

Thank you for the examples of Abraham and Sarah. Thank you for challenging me to believe that nothing is too hard for you. Thank you that you give me a lifetime to learn to walk in faith.

Amen

Settle down in the presence of the Lord and meditate on this question, "Is anything too hard for the Lord?" Reflect about whatever comes to mind. Take time later to contemplate the questions in Further Reflections and the Bible verses below. Remember the stages of lectio divina: read, meditate, pray and contemplate.

Is anything too hard for the Lord?

Further Reflections

1. What difficult, even impossible, situation have you faced and where was God in it? Does this question give you hope?

2. When have you experienced God doing something wonderful for you or someone you love?

Lectio Divina

Jeremiah 32:17

"Ah sovereign Lord, you have made the heavens and the earth by your great power and outstretched arm. Nothing is too hard for you."

Matthew 19:26

Jesus looked at them and said, "With man this is impossible, but with God all things are possible."

Chapter 12

What is the matter, Hagar?

The child grew and was weaned, and on the day Isaac was weaned, Abraham held a great feast. But Sarah saw that the son whom Hagar the Egyptian had borne to Abraham was mocking; and she said to Abraham, "Get rid of that slave woman and her son, for that slave woman's son will never share in the inheritance with my son Isaac."

The matter distressed Abraham greatly because it concerned his son. But God said to him, "Do not be distressed about the boy and your maidservant. Listen to whatever Sarah tells you, because it is through Isaac that your offspring will be reckoned. I will make the son of the slave into a nation also, because he is your offspring."

Early the next morning Abraham took some food and a skin of water and gave them to Hagar. He set them on her shoulders and then sent her off with the boy. She went on her way and wandered in the Desert of Beersheba.

When the water in the skin was gone, she put the boy under one of the bushes. Then she went off and sat down about a bowshot away, for she thought, "I cannot watch the boy die." And as she sat there, she began to sob.

God heard the boy crying and the angel of God called

to Hagar from heaven and said to her, "What is the matter, Hagar? Do not be afraid; God has heard the boy crying as he lies there. Lift the boy up and take him by the hand, for I will make him into a great nation."

Genesis 21: 8-18

This is Hagar's second conversation with the Lord (or his emissary), and the circumstances surrounding both conversations are similar. The first time Hagar fled, she ran away to escape Sarah's anger. This time, however, she has been sent away. Now she and Ishmael wander in the desert and they can't return home; they've run out of food and, more importantly, water. Hagar may have wondered why God had ever sent her back in the first place and why God has now allowed her to be exiled. She has lost all hope. Then the familiar voice said, "What is the matter, Hagar?"

Remember, Ishmael was not the child of the promise and Hagar was a slave. One might think God would not be concerned with either Hagar or Ishmael. Not true. They were both valuable to God. He asked Hagar what was the matter, and then the angel of the Lord continued, "Do not be afraid; God has heard..."

The very next thing that happened: God "opened Hagar's eyes," and she saw a water well (*v 19*). They were saved! Maybe the well had been there all along, but Hagar's tears blinded her. Or God saw their desperate need for water and his unseen hand had led them to the well. Maybe God knew where the water was and created the well on the spot. However it happened, Hagar had been blind and now she could see.

Perhaps in the exact moment when God asks, "What is the matter?" his provision is at hand. When we are open to God, when we hear his voice, when we tell him what is wrong—in that very moment—our salvation begins. In the instant we turn to him, God can open our eyes, too.

Water was not the only thing Hagar and Ishmael needed to survive. In dangerous territory for a single mother and child, they needed protection and they needed a plan. God stayed with them while they lived in the desert and the plan unfolded. Ishmael became an archer and later Hagar got him a wife. God reiterated his promise to make Ishmael into a great nation. He did not leave them to fend for themselves, but protected them for the rest of their lives.

Often times God seeks us when we are abandoned, alone, in hiding, or on the run. We need this question, "What is the matter?" for at least two reasons. The first reason is to know that something is the matter. The second is to grapple with what the matter really is. We have such a tendency to complicate simple matters, that when God asks a simple question, we have the opportunity to see ourselves and our story in a new light. Just telling God the truth, or what you think is the truth, can awaken new possibilities. Even if it's complicated, there may be a very simple first step.

Pause for a bit and savor the questions God has posed. Simple, mundane questions we ask each other every day. Where are you? What's so funny? Where have you been? Where are you going? God longs to connect with us, to be friends with us. He still remembers walking with us in the cool of day. When God asked this question, he didn't expect Hagar to give him a list of her problems. In a way, what he said was an announcement: "I'm here. You matter to me. Take comfort. Things will be more than okay."

The God of the universe notices this boy and his mother. He hears their cry and sees their dilemma. Have there been times when you have been upset and just wanted someone to notice and perhaps ask the same question of you? It is beyond comforting to know that God sees you when your heart is breaking, when you're alone and afraid, when you've lost everything.

I experienced this myself one time. Years ago someone wounded me and I couldn't get over it. I forgave, reconciliation followed, and I put the matter behind me. But in quiet moments, painful memories intruded and fresh sadness invaded my heart. It was like a dead volcano in my interior landscape that rumbled to life again every once in awhile and sent me reeling. After several years of this, I implored the Lord to heal me.

Not long after this prayer, I woke up in the middle of the night and once again painful memories flooded my mind. In my spirit I turned to the Lord and he said, "All that you went through—I saw it all." He conveyed great compassion. It was clear he wasn't taking sides or putting the other person down, but he wanted me to know he saw *me*. I felt very loved as a result of this encounter. To learn that God knew my pain and had compassion brought deep healing to me.

God does many unexpected things in Holy Scripture, but we often find him seeking those who are lost, those who are afraid, those who are powerful, and those who are powerless..

When hope is gone, God can open our eyes. All of a sudden, we see a well. We find just what we need in the nick of time. Maybe we can't go home again, but we can learn to live in this new place, even if it is a desert. We can even thrive. Sometimes what we need is not at all what we *think* we need. When we see no future, he promises one. When we are forlorn and despairing, he seeks and asks, "What is the matter?"

Prayer

Father,

I know what it's like to be blind to the well that is right in front of me, and what it feels like to have no safety net. Thank you that you see me, too, that when I cry, you see my tears. Thank you for your promise to be with me in the desert. I'm grateful you are my safety net.

Amen

Settle down in the presence of the Lord and meditate on this question, "What is the matter?" Reflect about whatever comes to mind. Take time later to contemplate the questions in Further Reflections and the Bible verses below. Remember the stages of lectio divina: read, meditate, pray and contemplate.

What is the matter?

Further Reflections

1. Is there a current situation that is a struggle for you? Or perhaps there is an old wound and no closure. Whatever comes to mind, tell the Lord about it. Write it in a letter to the Lord.

2. Sometimes we sense something is wrong, but we don't know what it is. Ask God to reveal anything that is hidden. Write down what you sense him saying.

Lectio Divina

Psalm 145:18-19
The Lord is near to all who call on him, to all who call on him in truth. He fulfills the desires of those who fear him; he hears their cry and saves them.

Psalm 147:3 (The Passion Translation)
He heals the wounds of every shattered heart.

Chapter 13

What is your name?

So Jacob was left alone and a man wrestled with him until daybreak. When the man saw that he could not overpower him, he touched the socket of Jacob's hip so that his hip was wrenched as he wrestled with the man. Then the man said, "Let me go, for it is daybreak."

But Jacob replied, "I will not let you go unless you bless me."

The man asked him, "What is your name?"

Genesis 32:24-27

In the scene described above, Jacob, the grandson of Abraham, had been wrestling with a mysterious stranger all night. A long backstory has brought Jacob to this place. Jacob and his twin brother Esau were Abraham's grandsons. Esau, as the first born, was destined to be the heir to all the promises God had made to Abraham: the land, the great nation, and the blessing that would be poured out on all nations through Abraham's descendant.

However, a prophecy also predicted that Jacob would inherit the birthright instead. Rather than waiting to see how this prophecy would be fulfilled, Jacob, who was an ambitious man, took the blessing by deception. He pretended to be his older brother Esau, and tricked his father Isaac to designate him as the heir. After Esau found out what Jacob had done, he threatened to kill him, so Jacob fled in fear of his life, heading to his uncle's home, a safe haven.

On the first night of his escape, Jacob camped under the stars and had a magnificent dream. Angels ascended and descended on a great ladder that stretched to heaven. Then God spoke. He promised to be with him, to watch over him, and someday to bring him back home. What was Jacob's response? *If* you will really do these things, *then* you will be my God. In other words, Jacob liked God's terms, but he wanted to see some proof. After this encounter, Jacob journeyed on to his Uncle Laban's home.

Uncle Laban turned out to be a bit of a trickster himself. Jacob wanted to marry his beautiful daughter Rachel, but Laban required seven years' work for him to win her hand. Then Laban switched Rachel for her homely sister Leah who was hidden behind a veil. This ruse was reminiscent of Jacob's own deception of his father when Jacob pretended to be Esau. After seven more years, Laban agreed to let Rachel marry Jacob.

In the meantime Jacob acquired flocks and herds and wealth, and soon decided it was time to take his wives, return home, face Esau and obtain his inheritance. Jacob believed Laban would try to stop him, so he sneaked away with his wives and all his possessions. Jacob was on the run again, this time from Laban. He faced (in the words of Jerry Garcia), "trouble ahead, trouble behind."

At this point in the story, Jacob was on the journey home. He was alone in the dead of night when the Angel of the Lord engaged him in the wrestling match. An intimate struggle, but still a struggle. At the break of day, still wrestling and exhausted, Jacob asked for a blessing.

The Lord's angel said to Jacob, "What is your name?"

Names in scripture are very important. Names mean something, often signifying a person's character or essence. A name can be prophetic. God changed the patriarch's name from Abram to Abraham (father of many) long before Isaac was born. God named Isaac "laughter" and Ishmael "he hears." If you know a person's name, then you know something about them, and in some sense, he has to answer to you.

The name Jacob means, "Deceiver," or "Grasper," and in the past he had proven true to his name. Did his parents see something in him to suggest this was a fitting name for their son? He did come out of the womb grasping his brother's heel, as if trying to get ahead of him. Did his parents take that as a sign of his personality? Did the name play a part in who he became?

For all his life Jacob had been identified as a trickster, a deceiver, a grasper. His name went before him; it stuck to him; he had become it.

The last person who asked Jacob his name was his father Isaac, on his deathbed. And Jacob lied. "I am Esau, your firstborn."

This time, with the angel, he told the truth. No more lies, no fig leaves. "I'm Jacob [I'm the deceiver]." Then the most surprising turn of events occurred. The angel said, "Your name will no longer be 'Jacob,' but 'Israel,' because you have struggled with God and man and overcome" (*Genesis 32:28*). And the name Israel—"one who struggles with God and man and overcomes"—became the name of Jacob's family, and ultimately, the name of God's chosen people.

The long night of wrestling with the angel of God was the culmination of all the struggles of Jacob's life, starting with wrestling with his twin brother in the womb. A metaphor for his life, this event also represents the future struggle of each and every person with God. Because in a way, we all have a bit of the deceiver in us. We all angle at times to get favor or special treatment. Our culture even trains us to position ourselves (ahead of others) for our promotions. We can be ruthless in that pursuit. Perhaps we require wrestling with God to grow at last into the person he created us to be. We struggle with God to discover, to be taught, and finally, to know our name—our true selves. The struggle transforms us.

With whom has Jacob struggled? For sure we know his brother, his father, his father in-law, himself, and God. What exactly has Jacob overcome? Not the angel of the Lord, who with one touch wrenched Jacob's hip out of its socket. Hasn't he rather overcome the voracious ambition that compelled him to get his way by any means? Hasn't he overcome his knee-jerk temptation to lie? All his years he has schemed to get what he wanted. The source of his blessing was for him to take. He even tried to bargain with God. "You do this for me, you will be my God." In the wrestling match perhaps he sees that the source of blessing is not the birthright, not the land or the inheritance of the firstborn, not the wealth he could gain by hook or crook; the source of his blessing is the Lord himself.

One more thing about names. Just before the saga of Abraham and his family began, a group of men in Babel decided to "make a name for themselves" by building a tower that would reach to the heavens. God scattered them across the earth and their plans came to nothing. We don't have a clue who these men might have been, and whoever they were, their names have long since been forgotten (*Genesis 11:1-9*). In the very next chapter of Genesis, God issued his call to Abraham. One of the promises God made to him was that he would make Abraham's name great. Think for a minute about how much time, energy, money, and talent is spent today for fifteen minutes of fame. Consider how many people wear designer logos as a name tag. Now think about how many thousands of people over thousands of years know and revere the name Abraham. We are busy making a name for ourselves; God is busy building us into our true name.

Jacob asked the angel of the Lord for a blessing and he received a whole new identity. God revealed who God knew him to be, who God created him to be. All along God saw something more in Jacob than his parents had seen when they named him or what his actions broadcast about him. It's as though God said, "Who are you really?"

Jacob said, "I'm the deceiver, always scheming, always grasping. This is who I am."

God responded, "Not anymore. Cast it aside. You are forgiven for deceiving your father. Now and henceforth, you will be who you really are. One who struggles, yes, but also one who overcomes." It has taken a long struggle for this identity to be birthed.

How would your own struggle change if you knew it was birthing in you your true name? How would it change if you knew, no matter what the struggle, God is in it, too, he is intimately involved with all the struggles of your life? How would you feel if you believed, if you just hang on until daylight, a blessing awaits, you too? Jacob knew something crucial about God, maybe learned through the old family stories. God's nature is to bless, and Jacob had the audacity to ask.

Prayer

Father,

You alone know the real me. Before my parents defined me, or my teachers or my friends, before my town, my church, my culture called me, you knew my very soul. You knew it before I could even imagine it. Before anyone was aware of my primitive beginnings, you saw me.

My children and my husband know me very well. And I can tell my friends all sorts of secrets. But you alone really know me. You have a name for me that transcends this particular moment in time.

I am who you know me to be. I am yours. I am a member of your family. I'm like everyone else. I am special.

In your remarkable world, everyone gets to be special. It is overwhelming. Thank you.

Amen

Settle down in the presence of the Lord and meditate on this question, "What is your name?" Reflect about whatever comes to mind. Take time later to contemplate the questions in Further Reflections and the Bible verses below. Remember the stages of lectio divina: read, meditate, pray and contemplate.

What is your name?

Further Reflections

1. Who or what have you struggled with in your life and what have you overcome?

2. Has anyone ever seen something crucial about who you are that gave you a new self-awareness or understanding, (a new "name")?

Lectio Divina

Isaiah 62:2b
You will be called by a new name that the mouth of the Lord will bestow.

*Revelation 2:17b (*The Passion Translation*)*
To everyone who is victorious I will let him feast on the hidden manna and give him a shining white stone. And written upon the white stone is inscribed his new name, known only to the one who receives it.

PART 3

MOSES
THE FRIEND OF GOD

Chapters 14 - 19

The Israelites grew from a large family into a huge tribe while they lived in Egypt as slaves. Then Pharaoh announced a new edict: kill all the Israelite baby boys. Moses' parents refused to comply with Pharaoh's cruel law. In hope of a rescue, they put their baby boy in a basket and set him adrift on the Nile River. Pharaoh's daughter found Moses, adopted him, and saved him from certain death.

So Moses grew up in Pharaoh's home amidst wealth and power. Later, as a young man, he wanted to help his downtrodden people. He "helped" by foolishly killing one of the Egyptian slave drivers and so became a wanted man. Moses then fled to the desert and settled in Midian.

We find him forty years later, tending sheep in the middle of nowhere, when he sees a burning bush, draws near it to take a closer look, and then his life takes an amazing turn. God spoke to him from the bush. He wanted to help his people, too, and Moses was, after all, the man for the job. Moses was to go back and demand the freedom of his people.

This is the story of how Moses forged the tribe of Jacob into the nation of Israel, but first God had to forge a relationship with Moses. We will see Moses become a man of deep faith in the context of his calling and destiny. We will also see the struggle of Moses and all the people living in the wilderness for years to come.

Before you move on to the questions in this section, think about faith, how your own faith has developed and your own time in the wilderness. Do you find a connection between faith and the wilderness experience? You may identify with Moses, who found himself on a mission he never planned for, or like the Israelites, who were saved and then led kicking and screaming into a freedom they weren't sure they wanted.

Chapter 14

What is in your hand?

"And now the cry of the Israelites has reached me, and I have seen the way the Egyptians are oppressing them. So now, go. I am sending you to Pharaoh to bring my people the Israelites out of Egypt."

… Moses answered, "What if they do not believe me or listen to me and say, 'The Lord did not appear to you?' "

Then the Lord said to him, "What is that in your hand?"

Exodus 3:9 and *4:1-2*

This question came to Moses from the burning bush. The voice, identified as I AM (YAHWEH, the Lord), gave Moses an instruction: travel back to Egypt, go to Pharaoh, and demand that his people, the Israelite slaves, be allowed to leave. Moses asked questions: Who am I to do such a thing? Who should I tell them sent me? What if they don't believe me?

Moses definitely didn't believe he was fit for the assignment. He couldn't imagine why Pharaoh would ever listen to him, even if he did convince him he spoke for the Lord.

God answered all Moses' questions, and then, as though to settle the matter, he asked Moses a question: "What is in your hand?"

Moses didn't have to look far or set out on a quest or find something magical to convince either his people or Pharaoh that it was really God who had sent him. He didn't have to pull a sword out of a stone to be a hero. God had a destiny for Moses, a great mission to accomplish. Moses didn't have to reinvent himself for God to use him. He didn't have to brush up on his speaking skills or go to school or get a degree. He didn't have to get certified or ordained. God could use what Moses already had in hand: in this case, a staff. The message was, whether Moses knew it or not, "You already have all you need."

With this staff Moses struck the Nile River and turned it into blood, the first plague. It was a sign to Pharaoh as well. Moses was a powerful contender. Using this same staff, Moses divided the Red Sea so the Israelites could escape the Egyptians.

Again, with this staff Moses struck the rock and water gushed out for the thirsty Israelites in the desert. Raising this staff high, Moses oversaw the Israelites defeat the Amalekites who attacked them in the desert. The staff was a sign to the Israelites and to their enemies, but it was a sign to Moses as well. God was with him. He empowered him to fulfill his mission. The staff was a tangible object demonstrating the faithfulness and power of God.

Sometimes when I read the Biblical accounts or hear about some modern day hero of the faith, I feel rather inadequate. I've never been on a dramatic mission in my life, but sometimes life itself thrusts you into the deep and even if you have the training for it, you know you're in way over your head.

I had just received a master's degree when I got a job at Rainbow Mental Health Facility in Kansas City. I was assigned a teenage girl who had had a terrible life. Her drug-addicted mother had prostituted this girl to get money for her drugs. She was taken from that home only to be placed with her father, whose new wife wanted nothing to do with her. Before being declared a ward of the state, she spent time at Rainbow Mental Health Facility where I became her therapist.

She sat in group therapy with a blanket over her head. When she saw me, she ran away from me. In private sessions she walked around my office never even making eye-contact and refusing to talk. My shiny degree and counseling techniques were no preparation for this. What did I have at hand? I really liked her. She was special, and I had an intuition that she liked me, too, though none of her behavior indicated so.

I started from scratch. When she ran away, I chased her. (Later, when I was on the playground with my own children,

I realized we were enacting a game that children love to play). I felt she needed touch, but how to do that? I took her to the drugstore, let her pick out some nail polish, and gave her a manicure. She liked it. She relaxed, and she began to chat.

By the time she was ready to leave Rainbow, she was articulate. She laughed, she made friends. She offered amazing insights. When she "graduated," I gave her a quilt with a picture of a rainbow on it. What did I have at hand? Nail polish, a game of chase, and a quilt. What I really had at hand, more than training and a degree, was true affection for a very unhappy girl and inspiration from the Holy Spirit.

Your job may look daunting: you don't have enough money; you're too old or too young; you don't have the resources, skills, or qualifications; you don't already know how to do it, or you're afraid people will think you're crazy or they'll judge you. Maybe you're not dreaming big enough.

Moses dreamed of helping his kinsmen. God dreamed of liberating them.

God can take what we already have and put it to work in useful, even amazing ways. If we focus on all the reasons it won't be enough, how do we dare begin? In fact, we won't even take the first step.

How many times have you had a passion or dream to do something, but you played the "yes/but game" until you talked yourself right out of doing anything? In what ways do you argue with God (or yourself) about why something won't work or about what you think you must have in order to accomplish the task before you?

This question is for you. What do you already have at hand? What slingshot and stones are you carrying in your back pocket?

Can you offer these things wholeheartedly to God, to be used for his purposes and see what happens?

What about Moses and his staff? He performed miracles before Pharaoh, parted the Red Sea, won battles in the desert, and turned bitter water sweet. The staff never left his side, and neither did God.

Prayer

Lord,

I thank you for all the gifts you have given me, especially for my friends, my husband, my children and my precious grandchildren. I thank you for my good mind and my sense of humor. Everything that I have comes from you.

But with all of these blessings, I still tend to think I don't have all I need, or I don't have enough. Sometimes I feel like an aging ingenue.

I am really sorry. In all these gifts, I see you are a great giver. You keep giving me yourself. That is truly full measure, pressed down, overflowing.

Amen

Settle down in the presence of the Lord and meditate on this question, "What is in your hand?" Reflect about whatever comes to mind. Take time later to contemplate the questions in Further Reflections and the Bible verses below.

What is in your hand?

Further Reflections

1. What gifts or possessions, spiritual or physical, do you most treasure?

2. What obstacles do you face and how has God already prepared you to meet the challenge?

3. What has God already given you to help you do great things?

Lectio Divina

Judges 6:14
The Lord turned to him [Gideon] and said, "Go in the strength you have and save Israel out of Midian's hand."

Deuteronomy 30:11-14
"Now what I am commanding you today is not too difficult for you or beyond your reach. It is not up in heaven, so that you have to ask, 'Who will ascend into heaven to get it and proclaim it to us so we may obey it?' Nor is it beyond the sea, so that you have to ask, 'who will cross the sea to get it and proclaim it to us so we may obey it?' No, the word is very near you; it is in your mouth and in your heart so you may obey it."

Chapter 15

Who gave man his mouth?

Moses said to the Lord, "O Lord, I have never been eloquent, neither in the past nor since you have spoken to your servant. I am slow of speech and of tongue."

The Lord said to him, "Who gave man his mouth?... Now go; I will help you speak and teach you what to say."

Exodus 4:10-11 & 12

Moses was still not convinced and argued further with God. He was sure he was not a powerful speaker, not persuasive enough to confront Pharaoh or lead the Israelites; he was sure God still had the wrong man.

Then God said to Moses, "Who gave man his mouth?" He did not wait for Moses to answer. He told him how the whole plan would work: "I will help you speak and teach you what to say."

Without a doubt, God knew what a "mouth" could accomplish. Moses' speaking talents and persuasive skills were not what made him useful to God, but he did need his voice. Moses needed God's help and instruction, not a class in debate or oral argument, and God needed Moses' faith and willingness to go.

The answer to God's question is, "You did."

So by implication God understood the gift. Since God gave Moses his mouth, maybe God knew what it was really for, more than Moses did—how powerful his words could be. Yes, God presented an overwhelming assignment, but his voice spoke from a burning bush, making promises to Moses.

Wouldn't this cause any of us to pause and consider that this mysterious voice, this "I Am," is more powerful than we can imagine? Wouldn't we be intrigued? Maybe, maybe not.

After all, God called Moses to go into territory where some might remember he was a wanted man. Some might recall he was himself an Israelite, and getting rid of him could be just the message Pharaoh would want to send to the slaves.

God called Moses to a risky mission, asked him to trust him in the process, and promisd he would do miraculous things to make the whole undertaking succeed. The one who gave man his mouth could also give him his voice. Surely this voice speaking from a burning bush could make good on his promise.

This was an invitation to a grand adventure, a noble call, and God himself would accompany Moses. After all these assurances, did Moses fall on his knees in awe? Did his soul expand with excitement? Did he say in all humility, "Let this be according to your word?" Did he pack his bag and prepare for the journey?

No. Instead Moses said, "O Lord, please send someone else to do it."

The surprising thing is, God didn't lose patience, he didn't call the whole thing off, he didn't even look for someone else for the task. In tolerance, God listened and then told Moses to take his brother Aaron with him, and God would help both of them speak to Pharaoh. And that is what happened.

God's imperturbability is so encouraging to me. He chose Moses. He saw something in him that Moses did not see in himself. And, despite Moses' objections, he talked Moses into the quest of a lifetime. God accommodated some of his concerns by including his brother. Moses didn't have to go alone.

Equally encouraging is the promise that God would help him and teach him what to say. God did not leave Moses stewing in doubt and unbelief. In spite of his initial reluctance, Moses grew into a great man with great faith. Together he and God accomplished an incredible deliverance. He would go on to lead the Israelites for forty years and establish them as the people of God. He remains, perhaps, the greatest leader of all time.

Implicit in this story is that God has good, sometimes exciting and even dangerous, intentions for us. If he does, he's committed and able to cause us to grow into the person who can complete the task. When we accomplish the goal or die trying, no one is more proud than God.

If Moses had persisted in his resistance, he would have missed it all. God was, however, even more persistent, and, of course, in the end Moses said yes.

What we don't know is what would have happened if he'd dug in his heels and spent the rest of his life herding sheep in Midian. I wonder how many have said "No" to God and then spent their lives in mild discontent, still loved by God, but missing their call to greatness.

When we are called to confront injustice or speak of God's power or love or truth, will not God also help us and teach us what to say? Moses told Pharaoh: "Let my people go." These were the very words God gave Moses, and thousands of people today could attribute these words to him. These words have been taken up by freedom fighters ever since. Moses may have dragged his feet, but he went and he delivered the message.

What followed was an amazing clash between Pharaoh, his priests—and their occult powers—and God's man Moses. Not until ten plagues were unleashed against the Egyptians did Pharaoh let them go. Moses held his staff over the Red Sea before the Israelites so they could escape. Forty years of miracles, wonders, and provisions in the desert followed. The ten commandments were established and the tabernacle, the design of the temple to come, was built.

At the end of his life, this is what was said of Moses:

Since then, no prophet has arisen in Israel like
Moses, whom the Lord knew face to face, who
did all these miraculous signs and wonders the Lord

sent him to do in Egypt—to Pharaoh and to all his officials and to his whole land. For no one has ever shown the mighty power or performed the awesome deeds that Moses did in the sight of all Israel.

Deuteronomy 34:10-14

Prayer

Lord,

I am all yours. I love this life and I love an adventure—at least, the idea of an adventure. And I want to live a life worthy of a great epitaph.

Amen

Settle down in the presence of the Lord and meditate on this question, "Who gave man his mouth?" Reflect about whatever comes to mind. Take time later to contemplate the questions in Further Reflections and the Bible verses below.

Who gave man his mouth?

Further Reflections

1. What God-given gifts do you have that you may have underestimated or discounted? What would you like to do with them?

2. Moses was not good with words (he believed), and part of the mission involved proclaiming God's word. Implicit in this story is that words can be powerful. What words spoken to you have been especially meaningful? Can you think of words you can speak to someone that might be important for them?

Lectio Divina

Acts 18:9-11

One night the Lord spoke to Paul in a dream. "Do not be afraid; keep on speaking, do not be silent. For I am with you, and no one is going to attack and harm you, because I have many people in this city." So Paul stayed for a year and a half, teaching them the word of God.

Matthew 10:19-20

"But when they arrest you, do not worry about what you say or how you say it. At that time you will be given what to say, for it will not be you speaking, but the Spirit of your Father speaking through you."

Chapter 16

Why are you crying out to me?

Then the Lord said to Moses, "Why are you crying out to me? Tell the Israelites to move on. Raise your staff and stretch out your hand over the sea to divide the water so that the Israelites can go through the sea on dry ground."

Exodus 14:15-16

After the last plague, after the first Passover, Pharaoh allowed the Israelites to leave Egypt. Then he changed his mind. The Israelites saw the Egyption army with six hundred chariots racing toward them, they were hemmed-in at the Red Sea, they were terrified, and they blamed the whole fiasco on Moses.

"Was it because there were no graves in Egypt that you brought us to the desert to die… Didn't we say to you in Egypt, 'Leave us alone; let us serve the Egyptians'? It would have been better for us to serve the Egyptians than to die in the desert!" (*Exodus 14:11-12*).

They were ready to give up.

Moses, however, had grown in faith and courage since his first encounter with God at the burning bush. He had seen God move mountains to get his people out of Pharaoh's clutches, so he was confident God would rescue them now. "Do not be afraid. Stand firm and you will see the deliverance the Lord will bring you today… the Lord will fight for you, you need only to be still" (*Exodus 14:13-14*).

Not only did Moses believe God would deliver them as he had before, he believed he knew how, so he ordered: "Stand!"

Then God said, "Why are you crying out to me?" and (or thereabouts) "Move! Raise your staff! Stretch out your hand! Take what you've got on hand. Divide the sea. Cross over."

Moses said, "Stand."

God said, "Move."

God's man got it wrong! I'm glad this scene is in the record.

It's a comfort to me because I can second-guess God and get things completely wrong, too.

God moved as well. A cloud that had been in front of the people shifted behind them and acted as their rear guard, hiding them from the enemy. Then Moses divided the sea, *a la* The Ten Commandments. He stretched out his arm over the sea, the Lord divided the sea with a strong wind and turned it into dry land, and the Israelites escaped (*Exodus 14:21-22*).

God's saved them in spite of their doomsday cries, their lack of faith, in spite of their blaming, complaining accusations, even in spite of their fear. For those of us who think we need to have the right attitude before God will help us, this story is an antidote. Or maybe just one person needs the right attitude. In this case, that person would be Moses.

What is the message in the question, "Why are you crying out to me?" Aren't we supposed to cry out to him? Maybe implicit in the question is the urgency of this moment. Now was not the time to entertain the Israelites' existential fears or their negative attitudes. Nor was it the time to wait (as Moses suggested).

Maybe God was just exasperated. They had so quickly lost faith, even after all the miracles they had witnessed. Maybe the question served as a splash of cold water to someone frozen in fear who needed to act now. Maybe it was not a question at all but God's way of saying, "We don't have time for this. You know what to do. *Do it!*"

Take a look at what the Israelites were saying. They were *not* pleading for help; rather they regretted their escape from Pharaoh and bemoaned their dire circumstances. They were intent on complaining while God was intent on saving them.

Maybe his question was an attempt to point out that they needn't wail at all. He was right there and he would save them.

Just when we think we have God figured out—what he will do and how he will do it—the land shifts under our feet. He tells us to move, but the next time he tells us to wait. We cry out and he comforts us and dries our tears. The next time he exhorts us. He might say something like, "Why are you crying? There's work to do."

And sometimes, often, he just remains silent. Maybe he thinks we already know what to do. God often encourages us to depend on him, wait on him, seek him, but here we see him saying something like, "What are you waiting for? Move! Get busy. You do it. Lean into the wind."

In the heat of the moment, when there's no time to consult the generals, the counselors, the priest, or our friends, God can communicate the fast action required, even if our legs are wobbly and we're convinced that defeat is imminent.

In a similar episode hundreds of years later, a king of Israel faced an invading army. The king called for a fast. He implored the Lord and then he received these instructions: "Do not be afraid because of this vast army. For the battle is not yours but God's... You will not have to fight this battle. Take your positions; stand firm and see the deliverance the Lord will give you, O Judah and Jerusalem. Do not be afraid; do not be discouraged. Go out to face them tomorrow, and the Lord will be with you" (*II Chronicles 20:15-17*).

God told Moses to spring to action. In the same way, God told the king in this later story, "Wait. Take your stand. I will handle this without your firing one shot. Just trust me."

How are you to know what to do when the enemy is

charging? It helps to have spent enough time with the Lord so you know his voice and his character. It helps to pay attention to what he's done in the past or what he's done for somebody you know. And if you don't really know his voice and the threat is upon you, listen anyway. God's voice often sounds like a hunch or an instinct.

We can't force God to speak in an audible voice, but we can practice listening. We can cultivate a conversation. We can be open and we can be still. We can experiment with God; sometimes taking a baby step and then waiting and listening, sometimes waiting and waiting until he opens the door and clears the path.

Sometimes we act in all boldness, next we bide our time. It becomes an intimate dance. We get no blueprint and the way forward is often not clear. We need to know God well so that, in an emergency, when time is of the essence, we recognize his voice and we obey.

The trick is not to project experiences from the past as a formula for what God will do tomorrow. It is about trusting and believing that God is really good and really strong and that he will show up.

I have a dear friend and spiritual mentor, who is now ninety-three years old. Over fifty years ago, she was suddenly widowed when her young beloved husband (a pastor) died of a heart attack, leaving two young children to raise by herself. She was overwhelmed with grief and with the daunting task before her. She was immobilized.

Here's what she did. At the top of every hour she poured two cups of coffee, one for herself and one for Jesus, and then she asked him what to do next. She would wait for a few minutes until she got a sense of what to do. She would then follow that prompting and do it. Sometimes that meant washing the dishes, sometimes making a decision about a job or finances, or maybe it was time to read to her children. This method got her through the immediate crisis and cemented for the rest of her life a deep, abiding, and intimate relationship with the Lord. She truly knows his voice.

Think about the times when you took matters into your own hands, the times you waited and waited and missed your opportunity, the times when quick thinking and fast action saved the day. Can you begin to see when you were protected by the hand of God, when you missed him altogether, and when you argued or complained?

Take heart because Moses and God's chosen people did it all.

Prayer

Lord,

I've cried out to you before when my situation seemed hopeless. Some of the time my prayers probably sound a lot like the Israelites' complaints.

But I wouldn't cry at all if I didn't have at least some hope that you hear me and you just might do something. It's such a relief that sometimes that is enough.

Amen

Settle down in the presence of the Lord and meditate on this question, "Why are you crying out to me?" Reflect about whatever comes to mind. Take time later to contemplate the questions in Further Reflections and the Bible verses below.

Why are you crying out to me?

Further Reflections

1. Do you seek God at the first sign of trouble or somewhere along the way? At the last possible moment? When hope is lost?

2. When have you experienced God coming through for you? Or have you ever experienced that? Is there a circumstance you are dealing with now that you could experiment with? Ask God to tell you what to do or how to see your circumstances from his viewpoint.

Lectio Divina

II Chronicles 20: 12 & 15
"For we have no power to face this vast army that is attacking us. We do not know what to do, but our eyes are on you."
This is what the Lord says to you: "Do not be afraid or discouraged because of this vast army. For the battle is not yours, but God's."

John 10:27
"My sheep hear my voice; I know them and they follow me."

Chapter 17

Is the Lord's arm too short?

But Moses said [speaking to the Lord], "Here I am among six hundred thousand men on foot and you say, 'I will give them meat to eat for a whole month!' Would they have enough if flocks and herds were slaughtered for them? Would they have enough if all the fish in the sea were caught for them?"

The Lord answered Moses, "Is the Lord's arm too short? You will now see whether or not what I say will come true for you."

Numbers 11:21-23

After a few months in the desert, the Israelites whined about the monotony of manna, the "bread" that God had provided each day. They were so unhappy that they wanted to return to Egypt and slavery (again) just to get a good dinner. Moses in turn complained to God about having to manage this unruly, rebellious, and discontented throng of people. Everybody but God was willing to throw in the towel.

In spite of all of the grumbling, God promised Moses he would send meat for everybody for a whole month. Moses responded, "There is no way!" And God said, "Let me show you how long my arm really is—I'll send enough quail for a month-long feast." And that is what happened.

Moses questioned whether God could accomplish something that God himself said he would do. The promise did not involve a miraculous victory over their oppressors. Neither salvation nor deliverance was involved. Who knew that God cared about providing something more than sustenance?

God is just and righteous, so when he sends Moses to set slaves free, we are not surprised. When he feeds them with manna in the desert so they won't starve, we are not surprised. In this story God sends quail, a delicacy, not because they needed it but because they wanted it. Many people preach that God is in the "business" of providing us only our needs, not our wants, and that we need to always be clear about the difference. Not this time.

We systematically think rewards (blessings) or consequences (punishments) are based on our worthiness. The Israelites did nothing to earn the quail; they didn't even have a good attitude.

But God showered them with this blessing—just like delivering them in the first place. God's ways are not our ways. He is way more lavish in his generosity, in what we call grace, than we are, unless we come under his influence. Maybe the gift was not just a blessing. Maybe it was designed to be an illustration revealing something about the giver: he really is good and he really is powerful.

In one way or another God posed this question, "Is the Lord's arm too short?" over and over because his people keep saying, in one way or another, "There is no way."

Maybe each generation needs to learn this lesson. Maybe many of us need a lifetime to believe that God will do extraordinary things for us. When our resources are scarce, when we are in the trenches, when we ourselves are in captivity, when there is no way out and we lose faith, God speaks, "Is my arm too short to save *you*?"

God repeats the question and reassures us with the answer. He speaks with patience, with loving-kindness, with vexation, and with power. Over and over in all kinds of situations, he tells us he loves us, he will help us, he will do what he says he will do, and he gives good gifts.

We hear about God's mighty works or we read about them, maybe even see some for ourselves, but when a new crisis erupts, our first thoughts are often fear, not faith. Or the monotony of a season of our lives wears us down and we fail to believe that God will do anything fresh for us. We start from scratch in the walk of faith again and again. Again and again we are invited to believe that God will come through for us.

In a prolonged time of financial drought, the Lord made a promise to me. He told me help was on the way, come back in a year about the matter, and, "It will be done."

You might think something that concrete, a word from the Lord, would settle the matter. I wish I could say I received this good news with gratitude and joy, and with patience and faith I awaited the provision.

Instead, I went through a litany of doubts. Was it really God who spoke to me or was it my wishful thinking and imagination? Was I supplying both sides of the conversation? I wasn't sure God was even in the business of financial aid. I wasn't convinced he cared about such mundane things, or that I was supposed to care about them either.

I continued in high anxiety about the future, but somewhere close to the mid-point, I took God at his word. In the sea of doubt, the original promise bobbled along like a little buoy and I felt hope.

A few more months with no sign of a breakthrough, new doubts erupted. What if God didn't do anything? Was I wrong not just about what I heard but about God as well? At last I cast out the doubts and, like a child clinging to her mother, I just held on to see what would happen. No matter what happened, I would cast my lot with him.

In the eleventh month, out of the clear blue, I found that a windfall from a former investment was forthcoming. Oh happy day! God came through for me! It was bring out the champagne, kick up my heels, celebrate, sing and dance time.

I was overcome with relief, but most of all I was in awe that God would make me a promise on his own initiative and keep it. I could, in fact, hear him. Above all, he had me in his sight, he cared for me. I learned that God does have a long arm.

Why does his love continue to surprise and astonish me? Why had I doubted? I fail to trust God because I don't know how good and generous he is. I don't know how powerful he is.

I do know how bleak the circumstances seem, how undeserving I am, how ordinary and embarrassing my problems are. I have been disappointed.

I wonder how the Israelites could whine and complain so much, and how often they were ready to head back to slavery just for a hot meal and the illusion of security.

I'm not so different. Maybe that's why all these stories are so cherished. Not because they make us feel superior, but because they're our stories, too.

The people we have been reading about had one encounter after another with God. God showed up in a garden, in a desert, in Pharaoh's palace and many other unlikely places. Over and over they were invited or admonished to trust and believe that when he made a promise, he would and could deliver.

There is one more aspect of this story as well. Maybe the gift of quail was also designed to teach his children something about their true selves. In spite of how radically we miss the mark, we were in the beginning designed to be just like God, extravagantly generous.

When you face the worst, be it financial calamity, sickness, addiction, divorce, even death, or anything under the sun, you can hear this challenge in your soul, the challenge to trust him, and come to believe, "Nothing is too hard for my God."

When you are just plain bored and in a rut, you might look around for some unexpected quail flying low to the ground. You can perhaps also hear the faint echo, "I am a great giver. I created you in my image. Be like me."

That's a blessing, too.

Prayer

Lord,

I know your arm is not too short, that no circumstance is beyond you. As great as that is, what I really appreciate is that not only can you save, but that you *want* to save.

And I thank you because you have shown up in my life over and over. Every good gift I have has come from your hand. I know you save. It's your job description. And I know I need a savior, so we are a perfect match.

Amen

Settle down in the presence of the Lord and meditate on this question, "Is the Lord's arm too short?" Reflect about whatever comes to mind. Take time later to contemplate the questions in Further Reflections and the Bible verses below.

Is the Lord's arm too short?

Further Reflections

1. Have you ever heard God speak a personal word to you, in your heart or in the scripture, or maybe through another person? What was your reaction? Did you take it seriously?

2. Do you long to hear from God? What are you doing to create a hospitable environment for him?

3. Think of three blessings that have come your way as sheer gift.

Lectio Divina

Isaiah 41:13
    For I am the Lord, your God, who takes hold of your right hand and says to you, "Do not fear; I will help you."

Zephaniah 3:17
    The Lord your God is with you
    He is mighty to save.
    He will take great delight in you,
    He will quiet you with his love,
    He will rejoice over you with singing.

Chapter 18

How long will these people treat me with contempt? How long will they refuse to believe in me, in spite of all these miraculous signs?

That night all the people of the community raised their voices and wept aloud. All the Israelites grumbled against Moses and Aaron, and the whole assembly said to them, "If only we had died in Egypt! Or in this desert! Why is the Lord bringing us to this land only to let us fall by the sword? Our wives and children will be taken as plunder. Wouldn't it be better for us to go back to Egypt?" And they said to each other, "We should choose a leader and go back to Egypt!"

Then Moses and Aaron fell face down in front of the whole Israelite assembly gathered there. Joshua son of Nun and Caleb son of Jephunneh, who were among those who had explored the land, tore their clothes and said to the entire Israelite assembly, "The land we passed through and explored is exceedingly good. If the Lord is pleased with us, he will lead us into that land, a land flowing with milk and honey, and give it to us. Only do not rebel against the Lord. And do not be afraid of the people of the land, because we will swallow them up. Their protection is gone, but the Lord is with us. Do not be afraid of them."

But the whole assembly talked about stoning them. Then the glory of the Lord appeared at the Tent of Meeting to all the Israelites. The Lord said to Moses, "How long will these people treat me with contempt? How long will they refuse to believe in me in spite of all the miraculous signs I have performed among them?"

Numbers 14: 1-11

Moses led the people through the desert right up to the border of the land God had promised to give to Abraham and his descendents. He sent twelve scouts to scope out the land to see what they might face when they moved in. They all reported that the land was beautiful, "flowing with milk and honey."

However, ten men reported that the cities were fortified, the people were strong, and giants were in the land; all but Joshua and Caleb told the people they were doomed. Panic ensued. Yet again, the Israelites grumbled and complained: "If only we had died in Egypt. Or in this desert!"

God saw their response, after all he had done, as a sign of contempt for him. Moses stepped in and pleaded on their behalf, he repented on their behalf, he argued with God on their behalf. God forgave, but with consequences.

This generation, who was too scared to take the land God had promised them, who repeatedly refused to trust God, would not enter the land; rather they would live as bedouins in the desert for the rest of their lives. God would continue to lead and protect them, but they would never enter Canaan.

Joshua and Caleb, the two who were convinced that, in spite of the giants, they could take Canaan with God's help, would eventually lead the next generation in victory and establish God's people in the land he had promised years before to Abraham.

God pointed out the real problem in the question he asked Moses. They *refuse* to believe. They have seen miracles, signs, and wonders. Why do they not believe? If seeing is believing, then they should be convinced by now. They've seen a river stop flowing, food appear out of nowhere, water pour from a rock, the cloud by day protecting them from the harsh sun, the fire at night guiding them, the very glory of God, not to mention the plagues back in Egypt that secured their deliverance.

Still they don't trust. They are ready to go back to Egypt. Better captivity than to risk their lives in this dangerous country. Better to be slaves.

The implication is that since they've seen a lot, they should have more faith, and since they don't, there are consequences. At this stage, their doubt progressed to something far worse. God called it contempt.

The question "How long will you refuse to believe in me?" implies that belief is a choice. That it's not just a matter of waking up and checking the faith thermometer. Faith comes with intention. Dare we admit there is an intention to doubt as well? At some point, failing to believe becomes *refusal* to believe, which can become contempt for God.

Centuries later Jesus encountered people who wouldn't believe in him. He performed miracles, healed everyone who asked for healing, turned water into wine as well as a few loaves and fish into a feast for thousands. But when the going got tough, many moved on, moved away, and lost faith. This does not even count the ones who became infuriated that he healed people on the wrong day. Many people in power saw his signs and wonders and had a vested interest in not believing. It's no different today.

If we are graced with signs and wonders and we explain them away or refuse to believe in God, then the consequences can be tragic. We, too, can live our lives in the desert, still fed by the hand of God all our days, but missing the greater blessing he intended to give us all along. Never to get home, never to enter the place of rest, never to fulfill our destiny.

What stands in the way of your faith? What issues do you wrestle with, wondering whether you can or should entrust them to God? Have you let your discouraging circumstances and your doubts determine your theory of what you think God will or won't or can or cannot do, or is his word itself your foundation?

Another important message is in this story. When we come out of captivity, we enter a new world that, while it is free, can also be confusing and wild. The Israelites had been slaves for a long time. First they had to unlearn a slavery mentality and then relearn how to live as free people. They had to embrace a new "free" identity.

Perhaps you remember a scene from the *The Shawshank Redemption*, about a man who had spent his entire adult life in prison. When he was finally released, he committed a crime just so he could return to prison. The world had changed so much while he was incarcerated that life back in prison seemed a much safer option. He had dreamed about his freedom, but now that he had it, all he wanted was to go back. That life was routine; he knew what to expect from that life. He wasn't free, but he knew the system and he had few responsibilities.

Even if we haven't been in prison, many of us have experienced other kinds of limitations, even captivity. When we are set free from our past, from our sins, from the demands of the false self, from bondage to drugs or toxic relationships, a whole new world to understand and adapt to awaits us, a new language to learn, new responsibilities to master. We find a new "free" identity to develop. It can be exhilarating, but I'm not so sure people today would fare better than these Israelites. Sometimes we keep returning to a life of bondage, especially when we are hurt or scared, because it feels safe and comfortable.

The land that God promised was a real, geographic place. It was a land of abundance, security, and rest for the Israelites. It was home. It is still a symbol for today: spiritual rest—a spiritual homeland in God, a spiritual place of beauty and freedom.

This is what we all stand to miss if all our grumbling and complaining shuts down our faith, or when the past captivity seems safer and easier than entering and conquering a new land, or when we are more comfortable with the cultural milieu rather than entering into an authentic relationship with God.

This theme of deliverance is the great theme of the Bible. God has determined to set us free from our captors, our enemies, even our own darkness and the lies we have believed about him and ourselves. He intends to set us free and get us to the Promised Land, the land flowing with milk and honey.

Prayer

Father,

I love it when life is going well and my own resources are adequate. I am full of gratitude for that.

But during those "good" seasons, it often doesn't occur to me to trust you. Sometimes I don't even ask your opinion of the course I'm taking.

Then life pulls the rug out from under me and I come running to you. It takes a while to get to the point of real trust. I keep reenacting in my own life the struggles your people experienced on the road to mature faith.

If I'm going to be a person of faith, then please make me a person of fierce faith. No more nambey-pambey faith.

Amen

Settle down in the presence of the Lord and meditate on these questions, "How long will these people treat me with contempt? How long will they refuse to believe in me, in spite of all these miraculous signs?" Reflect about whatever comes to mind. Take time later to contemplate the questions in Further Reflections and the Bible verses below.

How long will these people treat me with contempt?
How long will they refuse to believe in me, in spite of all these miraculous signs?

Further Reflections

1. Make an inventory of the times you have trusted God—and the times you haven't.

2. For every item in your "not trust" column, imagine what it might have been like if you had trusted God. How did it work out when you did trust?

3. What circumstances are difficult for you to entrust to God? Another way to ask this: Is there a worry that preoccupies you?

Lectio Divina

Deuteronomy 1:32-33

In spite of all this, you did not trust in the Lord your God who went ahead of you on your journey, in fire by night and in a cloud by day, to search out places for you to camp and to show you the way you should go.

Mark 5:36 & Mark 9:24

"Don't be afraid; just believe."

"I do believe; help me overcome my unbelief."

Galatians 5:1

It is for freedom that Christ has set us free. Stand firm, then, and do not let yourselves be burdened again by a yoke of slavery.

Chapter 19

Who are these men with you?

So Balak son of Zippor, who was king at the time, sent messages to summon Balaam son of Beor... Balak said:

"A people has come out of Egypt; they cover the face of the land and have settled next to me. Now come and put a curse on these people, because they are too powerful for me. Perhaps then I will be able to defeat them and drive them out of the country. For I know that those you bless are blessed, and those you curse are cursed."

The elders of Moab and Midian left, taking with them the fee for divination. When they came to Balaam, they told him what Balak had said.

"Spend the night here," Balaam said to them, "and I will bring you back the answer the Lord gives me." So the Moabite princes stayed with him.

God came to Balaam and asked, "Who are these men with you?"

Numbers 22:4-9

The Israelites were camped outside Canaan, near Moabite territory, and they were making the Moabite king nervous. But the Israelites were not interested in the Moabites; their sites were set on Canaan, the land promised to Abraham and his descendants. Having spent years in the desert, they were at last preparing to move into Canaan under the leadership of Moses' protégé Joshua.

Meanwhile, the king of Moab sent emissaries to a prophet named Balaam. The king wanted Balaam (who must have been good at this sort of thing) to pronounce a curse on the Israelites. The king believed a curse by this prophet would eliminate the threat. The men arrived and offered a deal to Balaam: we'll pay you to curse the Israelites.

That night while Balaam mulled over the proposal, God came to him and said: "Who are these men with you?"

Balaam explained the situation, and then God instructed Balaam not even to go with them, much less curse the Israelites because those people were, in fact, blessed. 'Do not curse what God has blessed' was the message, so Balaam declined to go and sent the men back to the king. However, the king sent more men with more money. They offered a larger payoff for Balaam, a bigger divination fee, and enticed him to go with them in spite of God's warning.

God's question was an attempt to interrupt Balaam, to cause him to give careful consideration to what he was about to do. No doubt, it was an attempt to get him to regard these emissaries from the king of Moab with a discerning eye. The question could have prompted Balaam to decide on his own that these men and their assignment were not for him. We learn he remained undecided because God warned him not to go with them at all.

I wonder how often we feel a twinge in our spirit, something like, "Maybe I shouldn't be hanging out with these people." And then, "I'm not really comfortable doing what they're doing." Or we get the admonition *"Do not go!"* but we go anyway.

This was a dire situation. It did not entail mere gossip or slander, both of which can be devastating; Balaam's words carried spiritual authority. The king's request and Balaam's "gift" treaded on dark, occult territory. It was witchcraft or black magic, and God took it seriously—it could have destroyed God's people.

This may be a far-fetched situation to modern readers (although occult practices still flourish). We may never find ourselves facing this kind of proposition, but it is certainly common to be tempted to go along with the crowd against our better judgment and to do the very thing we know is wrong.

Plenty of ways are available to curse someone other than through black magic. When we join in with others and curse or mock or bully or just gossip, the payoff is to become powerful, to become an insider, to profit in some way. We can assume superiority over the ones we curse and mock; we can feel powerful within the group; maybe we believe we can also gain protection against being "cursed" ourselves. Money may be in it for us, too.

We've all known people who bring out the worst in us. Companions can encourage a life of cursing or a life of blessing. Our associates determine a lot of our behavior. They can encourage us to curse others, to belittle them, or to wish them harm.

So God might say to us, "Who are you hanging out with?

What are you talking about? What are they talking you into?" The question suggests we have a responsibility to be wise, to pay attention to the twinge that registers deep inside and tells us to stop in our tracks or, at the very least, to be on guard.

Even our friends can entice us. What price do they offer and what price do you pay if you go with them? If you don't go? Have you ever felt God nudge you about your friends or maybe one companion in particular who sooner or later brings out the worst in you? Sometimes you want to be your honest, authentic self, but you make alterations to your true self in order to fit in. Maybe someone you spend time with often hurts your feelings. What entices you to stay in the relationship? The real question is this: do your companions encourage you to live a life of blessing or cursing?

Here is the rest of the story. God allowed Balaam to go with the men but warned him to say only what he told him to say. Then, worried that Balaam was not going to obey him, God sent an angel to block his path. Balaam couldn't see the angel, but his donkey could and refused to move forward, despite Balaam's whippings.

At last the Lord caused the donkey to talk to Balaam. She asked him why he kept beating her. Balaam explained that she was making a fool of him. The donkey said, "Am I not your own donkey, which you have always ridden to this day? Have I ever been in the habit of doing this to you?"

When Balaam answered, "No," the Lord opened his eyes so that he, too, could see the fierce angel. The angel then informed him that his donkey had saved his life. If she hadn't stopped, "I would certainly have killed you by now, but I would have spared her." (*Numbers 22:33*).

The angel allowed Balaam to keep going, but warned him

again to say only what the Lord told him. Much chastened, Balaam proceeded to the king and told him he could only speak what God put in his mouth. He then pronounced blessings over the Israelites, not curses, and not once, but three times.

God asked a question, sent an angel, made a donkey talk, opened Balaam's eyes to the precariousness of his situation, and in a stern voice commanded him not to curse the Israelites. Who knew that cursing God's people was taking your life in your hands? Who knew that pronouncing a curse carries such power that God would send an angel to stop it? When Balaam quit beating his donkey and answered her question, the veil was drawn back so that Balaam could see what was really going on. His very life was at stake.

How would you proceed if you could see the angel of the Lord, sword in hand, blocking your path and issuing a severe warning? This is a cautionary tale. If God asks us who our companions are, he may expect us to be discerning about them. He may expect us to stop seeing some of them. If we ignore a gentle question, we may remain blinded to our own precarious situation.

Prayer

Lord,

Help me discern who is good for me and who isn't. Help me to be strong enough to do right no matter who I'm with. Help me to set good boundaries where I need to. Help me to love all the people in my life with wisdom.

I never want to pronounce a curse. Please show me how to bless and be a blessing.

And one more thing, please put a shield around me and my family that no curse may ever fall on any of us.

Amen

Settle down in the presence of the Lord and meditate on this question, "Who are these men with you?" Reflect about whatever comes to mind. Take time later to contemplate the questions in Further Reflections and the Bible verses below.

Who are these men with you?

Further Reflections

1. What do you think counts as a curse? As a blessing?

2. Think of ways to bless your family or friends. Write down what comes to mind.

3. Do you have a friend who is like the donkey in this story, seeing things you don't yet see, warning and protecting you, putting on the brakes before you are tempted to do the wrong thing?

Lectio Divina

Psalm 1:1
    Blessed is the man who does not walk in the counsel of the wicked or stand in the way of the sinners or sit in the seat of the mockers.

Proverbs 4:14-15
    Do not set foot on the path of the wicked or walk in the way of evil men. Avoid it, do not travel on it; turn from it and go on your way.

Matthew 12:36-37
    "But I [Jesus] tell you that men will have to give account on the day of judgment for every careless word they have spoken. For by your words you will be acquitted, and by your words you will be condemned."

PART 4

BUILDING A NATION

Chapters 20 - 26

After nearly forty years in the desert under the leadership of Moses, the Israelites were ready at last to move into the land promised to Abraham over four hundred years before. The time in the desert had been important in their transformation from a tribe of slaves to a strong and more cohesive nation. The law and the blueprint for their religious life, given to Moses, was established, and now Joshua took over the reins to lead them into Canaan.

As they made their preparations, God spoke words of instruction and encouragement to Joshua. This is the summation of all God said to him: "Do not be afraid... Have courage!" (*Joshua 1*). They'd had a failure of courage the first time they came to the border of Canaan. Plus, the Egyptians had oppressed and dominated them. God knew if they continued to see themselves as victims they could easily give up and be enslaved again. It takes courage to cross into a land inhabited by people who would likely fight them at every turn.

It also takes courage to shed an unfortunate and misdirected self-image, the image of a downtrodden and oppressed people.

God knew that fear and lack of courage could doom them to another forty years in the desert.

Before you move on to the next questions, meditate for a few minutes on "courage" and what it means to you. Consider the times when you've been courageous as well as times when fear won the day.

Chapter 20

Stand up! What are you doing down on your face?

And Joshua said, "Ah, Sovereign Lord, why did you bring this people across the Jordan to deliver us into the hands of the Amorites to destroy us? If only we had been content to stay on the other side of the Jordan! O Lord, what can I say, now that Israel has been routed by the enemies? The Canaanites and other people of the country will hear about this and will surround us and wipe out our name from the earth. What then will you do for your own great name? The Lord said to Joshua, "Stand up! What are you doing down on your face?"

Joshua 7:7-10

God had chosen Joshua to lead his people after Moses died. His mission was bold—cross the Jordan River and lead the people into Canaan. The land was "flowing with milk and honey" but also with other tribes (including giants) who were fierce combatants.

As Joshua took the reins of leadership, God told him: "I will give you every place where you set your foot... As I was with Moses so I will be with you: I will never leave you or forsake you... Be strong and courageous... Be strong and very courageous... Be careful to obey all the law my servant Moses gave you... Be strong and courageous. Do not be terrified, do not be discouraged, for the Lord your God will be with you wherever you go." (*Joshua 1:3-9*).

Not long after God spoke these bracing words, we find Joshua at the apex of *dis*couragement, face in the mud, after a lost battle. What happened?

Joshua had already led the Israelites on an extraordinary military campaign. They marched around Jericho, the walls collapsed, and they captured the first city in the promised land. They acquired gold and silver and dedicated it to the Lord. They were ready to take the next city, which, according to all of the reports, would be an easy win.

Instead the Israelites were defeated and their heroic reputation, obtained after the battle at Jericho, was in tatters. Joshua, the spy who forty years before had absolute faith that with God's help they could defeat any enemy, lost his confidence. He lay prostrate on the ground in front of The Ark of the Covenant, and he cried out to God.

You might think this was the right response, that God would want Joshua to grovel before him. Instead God said, "Stand up! What are you doing on your face?" (Implied: "Remember what I just told you about courage!")

Next, God explained to Joshua what to do. He must consecrate or purify himself, in fact everyone must be purified, in preparation for meeting with the Lord. In effect, God told Joshua: "This is not the time for groveling. Get up. Dust yourself off. You—all of you—get clean inside and out. Prepare to meet with me. I'm going to tell you what is wrong and what to do."

Then God explained to Joshua why his army had become so vulnerable. After they defeated Jericho, someone had taken for himself some of the gold and silver which was supposed to be dedicated to God. Joshua had not done anything wrong, but, unbeknownst to him, his army had been corrupted by one bad man. That man would have to go.

Winning in battle was not the only thing on God's mind. He called the Israelites to holiness and he meant it. God allowed no compromise for this offense or for the offender. After the renegade had been dealt with, God repeated his earlier admonition to the shaken people, "Do not be afraid and do not be discouraged." Then Joshua and his men proceeded to capture the city, and this time God instructed them to keep all the gold for themselves.

One defeat can ravage us, no matter how much success we have chalked up in the past or how bravely we have fought in previous battles. One failure can be paralyzing. Like Joshua, we can end up with our faces in the dirt. Our internal dialogue might sound like this. "We thought God was fighting for us and with us, but now we are not so sure. We're on our own and it's looking grim."

If we don't have self-confidence, or God-confidence, we give up. Or we might act just like Joshua, begging God to help, or like the Israelites, reiterating the old refrain: "We should have stayed in Egypt, better to be slaves than perish in this godforsaken land." In his discouragement Joshua completely forgot he doesn't have to beg God at all. God made promises. God chose him to lead. God loves him. He's still on his side.

Joshua was new at leading and his army didn't have much experience. God wanted to show Joshua, as he had shown Moses and Abraham, how to be a man of faith and how to collaborate with God. This defeat provided a necessary lesson for them all. We all get discouraged no matter how many times God tells us not to. We all lose heart. We fall flat on our face. But this holy God does not require us—nor does he even want us—to cower before him. This defeat was such a time, a time to stand, inquire, obey, and to put aside discouragement.

We don't know why the person who took the gold for himself did it. Perhaps it was just greed, or his own little insurance policy, in case Joshua failed in this military campaign. Maybe gold was his idol and he just couldn't help himself.

Many of us have harbored a little forbidden gold for ourselves just in case God doesn't come through for us, or just because gold is our idol, too. This man brought failure to his friends and comrades because, as a group, they were to honor God for their victory. His greed and dishonesty backfired and caused the Israelites this defeat as well as his own demise.

Perhaps this is not a group problem for you but something

more personal. Instead of a bad apple in the group, what if the bad apple is in you? Do you have one weakness, one area where a temptation trips you up every time, an area where sin grows and gains momentum in your life, much to the ruin of your relationships and your true desires? Or perhaps one special way you sabotage yourself over and over again?

As he did with Cain, God might call on you to master your anger (or greed, jealousy, lust or unbelief), before it masters you. Like the Israelites, you yourself might need a time of cleansing. If doubt and discouragement cause your failure, then you, like Joshua, might be overcome by fear and dread. That fear will derail your best laid plans.

If you treat the sin like a cancer that can devour you, you will not rest until it is obliterated. Fear and doubt can do the same.

Here's what God has shown me about fear. While my husband was in recovery from emergency brain surgery, I became consumed by fear, doubt, worry, and anxiety. I became very discouraged. Not about his health and recovery—somehow I had faith for that —but about the consequences for our future. I didn't pocket any gold, but I thought, "It's all up to me. I must be on the lookout at all times for problems. I have to be ready to fix anything that goes wrong."

In taking all the potential hazards on my shoulders, I made myself the god of the situation and my burden grew. As I looked for problems, problems were all I saw; the more problems I saw, the more my anxiety grew. And to a degree, after a while, some things did fall apart.

My prayers became prayers of worry, not faith. I groveled. I repeated my worries and fears to God with no real hope that he would/could do anything. My "prayers" sounded just like Joshua's prayers: "Why did you let this happen? We're going to be wiped out. We're not going to make it." My burden and fear gripped me, and it was awful.

Many people decide at this point that God really cares, he just can't do much. He's very compassionate, but he has set up the universe to run without his intervention or even his help. Maybe there's a heaven when we die, but for now we really are on our own. These constructive atheists have at least two choices:

1. redouble their efforts to tackle all their problems using their own wits and resources, or
2. give up and accept the failure, injustice, loss (the "cancer"), as inevitable.

Others decide the sovereignty of God explains everything that happens; his will is always done and our part is to submit. This flies in the face of the Lord's prayer: "Thy will be done." Why are we to seek his will and pray for it if it is already a certainty?

At any rate, the solution for Joshua was my solution, too. I needed a purge. In a way God told me, like he told Joshua, to stand up, to quit acting defeated before this "enemy" (in my case the fear itself). My doubt and unbelief were really a lack of trust in God, so I repented. Not only was I sorry about it, but I changed my mind. I consecrated my imagination and banished all the fear and anxiety, including the lie that kept repeating in my soul, "You're not going to make it."

I read the word of God instead of stewing in my dark thoughts. I renounced all the lies that fed my anxiety, and I cast my fate on the Lord. I listened to him. I worked at trusting him. I commanded the spirit of fear to leave and never come back, and it worked! I found peace—tentative, at first—because worry had become such a habit.

Bit by bit, the shalom peace of God filled my thoughts and heart and made room for faith in God, instead of faith in myself, my agendas, formulas, and solutions. God had a victory in store for me, a victory without and a victory within.

Joshua needed to know again that, in spite of this defeat, he could still count on God. God would instruct him about what caused the defeat and what to do about it. And God gave him four messages (at least):

1. Consider external causes for what you take to be your defeat.
2. If you've lost your courage, you must get it back. It is crucial.
3. Sometimes you need a cleansing, a purge, or a consecration.
4. Today and yesterday are going or gone. Start anew; listen to me. I'll tell you what to do and what you need to know.

God needed a man who could cooperate and participate with him. He needed Joshua on his feet, clear-headed, ready and willing to listen and follow.

If you feel confident that God has called you to a task, but it falls apart and you find yourself flat on your face before the Lord, then this is a story of hope. If you find yourself in a vulnerable situation and you become obsessed with worry and eaten up with anxiety, this story might point you back to God and to courage. It may be time to remember that God wants all his children to be courageous. You might take a breath and remember that God is on your side and he's calling you to be by his side, too.

Prayer

Lord,

I love your admonition to be be very courageous and to fear not. Usually when you say that, I think I have very good reasons to be afraid. It feels like I can't control how I feel.

Then you repeat: "Do not be afraid."

Thank you for this word, because I've learned it's possible to obey. I also see from the way you deal with your people that a defeat does not mean that you have turned against me.

Thank you that you call me to be an overcomer. I truly want to serve you well.

Amen

Settle down in the presence of the Lord and meditate on this question, "What are you doing down on your face?" Reflect about whatever comes to mind. Take time later to contemplate the questions in Further Reflections and the Bible verses below.

Stand up! What are you doing down on your face?

Further Reflections

1. What failure in your life still causes you shame or regret? Did fear or discouragement play a part? Trace back to the root of it.

2. Have you experienced God guiding you out of failure and into victory? What part did courage play?

Lectio Divina

Ezekiel 2: 1-3

He said to me, "Son of man, stand up on your feet and I will speak to you." As he spoke, the Spirit came into me and raised me to my feet, and I heard him speaking to me.

Joshua 23:14

Now I am about to go the way of all the earth. You know with all your heart and soul that not one of all the good promises the Lord your God gave you has failed. Every promise has been fulfilled; not one has failed.

II Chronicles 32:7

"Be strong and courageous. Do not be afraid or discouraged because of the king of Assyria and the vast army with him, for there is a greater power with us than with him."

Chapter 21

Am I not sending you?

The angel of the Lord came and sat under the oak at Ophrah that belonged to Joash the Abiezrite, where his son Gideon was threshing wheat in a winepress to keep it from the Midianites. When the angel of the Lord appeared to Gideon, he said, "The Lord is with you, mighty warrior."

"But sir," Gideon replied, "if the Lord is with us, why has all this happened to us? Where are all his wonders that our fathers told us about when they said, 'Did not the Lord bring us up out of Egypt?' But now the Lord has abandoned us and put us into the hand of Midian."

The Lord turned to him and said, "Go in the strength you have and save Israel out of Midian's hand. Am I not sending you?"

"But Lord," Gideon asked, "how can I save Israel? My clan is the weakest in Manasseh, and I am the least in my family." The Lord answered, "I will be with you, and you will strike down all the Midianites together."

Judges 6:11-16

The Israelites settled in the Promised Land at last. Perhaps they envisioned all their troubles would be over once they had obtained this long-sought dream. But they had a problem. Their neighbors, the Midianites, swooped in at every harvest and pillaged their crops. The Israelites were helpless.

Gideon, a young Israelite, hid from them, threshing his wheat in secret and scared to death. This is the story of God commissioning an ordinary young man to lead a small band of Israelites to deal with the gangsters next door, making him a mighty warrior in the process. When an angel of the Lord first appeared to Gideon in his hideout, he said, "The Lord is with you mighty warrior."

The important thing Gideon needed to know was this: Things are not what they seem. In spite of your hard luck and many defeats, God is with you; in spite of your fear, you are powerful.

Gideon, like many before him, argued with God. In effect, Gideon said, "How can I save Israel? My family has nothing and I am the least of the bunch. Besides, if you were really with us, this wouldn't be happening. We've heard about your miracles in the past, but what have you done for us lately?"

Gideon posed the questions we all ask or at least think about deep down:

Lord, if you are so powerful, and so good and if you are truly our God, then why have you let all these terrible things happen?

Either you must not be so powerful, you must not be so good, or you must not really care about me or the injustice that is being done.

God brushed Gideon's questions aside. Instead he said, "Am I not sending you?"

From God's point of view, it was settled: Gideon and his men would defeat Midian.

Gideon had zero faith. He knew he was not a mighty warrior, no matter what this angel of the Lord said. He felt totally inadequate to the task. God, however, was the one sending him. All the excuses, the humiliations of the past, all the reasons why it wouldn't work, are, or should be, silenced. Gideon could not picture himself as a mighty warrior. He was mistaken.

Also, God promised to go with him. Gideon needed to *believe* that. And he had to choose to believe that what God told him about himself was far truer than what he believed about himself. This is the essence of faith: believing what God says in spite of the circumstances or experiences that would convince us otherwise. Gideon could only see a bleak future, when in reality God planned to make him a hero.

So Gideon gathered as many troops as he could. Then God told him his makeshift army was too big, and he cut it down in size, twice! God told Gideon to go and save using the strength he had. God's reason? "Am I not sending you?"

What did God want Gideon to realize? This question was not necessarily a promise about the outcome, but it did point out who was doing the sending. When *God* sends, he empowers. When he sends, he blesses the mission. His presence goes with the one he sends, just as it did with Jacob, Moses, and Joshua.

Now it was Gideon's turn. Gideon's true identity and his destiny have been revealed. He is mighty. He is a warrior.

Gideon was not convinced yet. He asked God to take a test

to make sure he would really do what he said he would do. And God took Gideon's test!

> Gideon said to God, "If you will save Israel by my hand as you have promised—look I will place a wool fleece on the threshing floor. If there is dew only on the fleece and all the ground is dry, then I will know that you will save Israel by my hand as you have said," And that is what happened…Then Gideon said to God, "Do not be angry with me. Let me make just one more request. Allow me one more test with the fleece. This time make the fleece dry and the ground covered with dew." That night God did so. Only the fleece was dry; all the ground was covered with dew.
>
> *(Judges 6: 34-40)*

With great patience, God did what seemed impossible in order to convince Gideon to believe. God's goal was to make Gideon a man of faith, as well as a mighty warrior. This is so foundational that God went through all the fleece and dew business so Gideon would really believe him.

The story ends well for Gideon and the Israelites. They defeat the Midianites. Gideon is hailed as a hero and he leads Israel for years to come.

I pride myself on being a make-it-happen kind of person. But if God sent me on a mission, taking on an enemy who bullied my family and friends, an enemy stronger than all of us, an enemy who terrorized us, I would look for a way out. After I got done arguing with God about the whole mess and how it was kind of his fault anyway, I might devise a plan.

I would start by raising money and gathering an arsenal. I

would call a meeting with all my allies and develop plan "A," plan "B," and plan "C." I might lobby my congressman for a new law. I would for sure sue somebody. And, oh yes, I might start a prayer chain.

If, after all that planning and delay, God said to me, "Go in the strength you have. Am I not sending you?", my faith would be on the line. I'd like to think I would go.

Sometimes like Gideon we find ourselves living in the promised land, (we graduated, got married, had the long awaited child, got the promotion) only problems arise which we hadn't anticipated. The new boss is difficult and the job is more stressful than we imagined it could be. Your husband has baggage. The children squabble.

These issues are minor, but serious problems catch us off guard and we can draw conclusions about God based on the problems. Like Gideon, we can have a nemesis who keeps tripping us up just at the point of success; the whole "promised land" seems full of potholes with one problem after another. Maybe we, too, believe there's nothing we can do and so, like Gideon, we hide out.

Despite your best effort, do you have little to show? Does an enemy charge in on schedule to steal your harvest? Your security? Your joy?

Maybe you hide out just trying to get through a difficult situation unnoticed, or you have lost hope for a different future. You might long for a mission. You want your life to count, but you can't see how or where to start. You can't see in yourself what God sees in you. You're not at all sure God will really back you up if you are called or thrust into a mission for him, or if he has now placed you right where he wants you.

Maybe your circumstances are your mission. You might

be feeling pretty sorry for yourself when God is calling you a mighty warrior.

Also, like Gideon, we often want a sign from God or confirmation of the word we think we've received from him. God's word to us can be ephemeral, and we are often not quite sure it was God who spoke or prompted. We're not sure the words in scripture apply to us. God did not begrudge Gideon's request for a sign. He knows sometimes that is just what we need.

After my mother's death, it was my job to clean out the house my parents had lived in for over fifty years. Each trip home involved laborious physical and emotional work in the clearing of closets, photographs, sorting through sentimental items, and deciding what to keep. My work was lonely but also cathartic.

One day, when I was working in the garage, I "saw" (in my mind's eye) my mother and daddy looking at me with huge smiles. They gazed at me with pride and love. I asked God if they were, in some sense, present. Later that day, the song, "Oh Happy Day," came on the radio. Then the next day, as I was driving back home to Austin, the same song again came on the radio. I noticed and I smiled and thought it a nice coincidence.

The following day I went to my usual exercise class, and at the end, the smiling instructor drummed on the floor and called out, "Oh Happy Day." Then I knew God had indeed heard me. He gave me a glimpse of my parents' smiling, unlined faces. That sign filled me with love for him for his kindness for me. Any sign from God, even if it's subtle or has to be repeated three times to be believed, is very special.

Your turn may come, and if you don't know your identity or destiny, then that could be your starting point. If you don't have faith, then ask for some. That itself can be a risky, courageous request. You may need to know whether the mission you have in mind is, in fact, the mission God calls you to. You might even start by being as audacious as Gideon and asking God to show you he is really with you by way of a sign.

You might even come to believe that if God calls you, it's because he believes in you. What an amazing thought.

Oh. Happy. Day.

Prayer

Lord,

I love being a mighty warrior. I also love sitting very still and waiting for you. My problem sometimes is figuring out which posture to take.

Please give me the eyes to see what you are doing and how you are calling me to participate. And if you are of a mind, I'd really like a visit from an angel, too.

Amen

Settle down in the presence of the Lord and meditate on this question, "Am I not sending you?" Reflect about whatever comes to mind. Take time later to contemplate the questions in Further Reflections and the Bible verses below.

Go in the strength you have. Am I not sending you?

Further Reflections

1. God told Gideon to go in the strength he had. What strengths do you have?

2. Have you ever experienced a confirmation from God about something he said to you?

3. Has God ever tapped you for a mission? Do you see a potential mission in your current circumstances?

Lectio Divina

Isaiah 41:9-10
> I took you from the ends of the earth,
> from its farthest corners I called you.
> I said, 'You are my servant';
> I have chosen you and have not rejected you.
> So do not fear, for I am with you;
> do not be dismayed, for I am your God.
> I will strengthen you and help you;
> I will uphold you with my righteous right hand.

Psalm 18:35
> You give me your shield of victory
> and your right hand sustains me;
> you stoop down to make me great.

Chapter 22

How long will you mourn?

Until the day Samuel died, he did not go to see Saul again, though Samuel mourned for him. And the Lord was grieved that he had made Saul king over Israel.

The Lord said to Samuel, "How long will you mourn for Saul, since I have rejected him as King over Israel?

I Samuel 15:35-16:1

Until now, Israel had not had a king, but all the nations around them had kings, so Israel wanted one also, a dynamic, exciting, and handsome leader. Samuel the prophet was God's right-hand man, and so Samuel was the one who anointed Saul as king. Samuel loved Saul, he mentored him, and believed that together they would be the military and spiritual leaders of Israel.

But Saul, though he looked good on paper, proved to be weak. He pandered to his troops, and he disobeyed and disrespected Samuel. He was a man after the hearts of men, not the heart of God. Saul had been a great military commander, but he failed to follow the instructions of God and his prophet Samuel.

Here's what happened the first time: Saul was to lead his troops into battle but delay attacking the enemy until Samuel arrived and performed the religious sacrifice. The men grew impatient so Saul performed the religious sacrifice himself, even though he had no authority to do so. This resulted in a warning. Later Saul kept booty, which was supposed to be destroyed, so he could pass it out to his men—once more so they would like him. He feared (desired) their approval more than he feared (desired) the approval of God.

Saul might not have known it at the time, but this was a test, and he failed. He was supposed to be a strong leader, do the right thing, and respect the authority of Samuel. He couldn't lead if he cared too much about being liked. He couldn't expect his men to do the right thing if he was too weak to do it, too.

It's interesting that God decided to end Saul's career as

leader after two mistakes, even though he gave to other leaders multiple opportunities to shape up. Moses, Joshua, and Gideon all argued with God, got things wrong, and failed in their duties, but God never gave up on them.

I note two things:

1. There is no recorded conversation between Saul and God, and
2. He made a mistake the others did not make, namely, he cared a lot more about what others thought about him than what God thought.

Samuel told Saul that the kingdom would one day be torn from him, and from that time until the day he died, Samuel never saw Saul again. He followed God's instruction, but still he felt like he'd lost a son. He was deeply saddened. Samuel grieved a loss not caused by death but rather by the death of their relationship and the death of his vision—his dreams for Saul and for the nation. Saul had to go, and Samuel knew it. The problem was that, in spite of Saul's weakness and disobedience, Samuel still loved him and he mourned his loss.

At some time, we don't know when, God asked Samuel how long he would grieve. Nothing about this question suggests Samuel's grief was uncalled for. Since we don't know how long Samuel had been grieving, neither is this question suggesting a guideline about how long grief should last.

And the passage doesn't include Samuel's response. We don't know if he said or thought something like, "I really need a few more months to process this," or "I can't even fathom how to go on from here. I was sure Saul was the one, and I'm just so disappointed." Whatever Samuel thought, God had a new mission that only Samuel could perform, so the question was at least a hint that he needed to be or become available to God.

We all suffer through many kinds of deaths and multiple griefs: a divorce, a broken friendship, a lost job, a prodigal child, and, of course, the death of a loved one. We can grieve the dreams we dreamed when we were young that fail to come true, the dreams we had for our old age that just don't pan out, the loss of status when our career ends, the continuing grief over past sins or foolish mistakes that robbed us of something we cherished. Nostalgia for the past can morph into grief for days gone by.

At any point along the way, we can get stuck in our grief, which can interrupt our lives for long periods of time. We become unavailable to our families, our work and to God. We can bury sadness so deep that when it erupts, not only are we plunged back into grief, but we are shocked by it, too. When we face catastrophic loss, grief can move into the core of our being and set up residence. I'm not suggesting any kind of timeline for grief to run its course, but perhaps the question God asked Samuel suggests that the immobilization that comes from grief can have an ending.

The road to healing can take surprising turns. I have a friend who faced every parent's nightmare; he lost a child. Time, the great healer, passed, but it did no good. He could not move on. He was swamped in heartache.

Then an interesting thing happened. He went on a religious retreat (which didn't do much good either), but on the last day the retreat leader approached him and suggested an assignment. He told my friend to spend a year finding joy, to look for it every day: "Do something every day for a year that brings you joy." After a year he was to come back on retreat.

With the assignment, and with the permission that came with it, my friend allowed room for joy. He took up cooking and became an excellent chef. He invited friends over for feasts he prepared. He spent time in nature. He resumed biking. He became available again to his wife and his other children.

At the end of the year, he was in a different place; he found he was strong again. He could carry his grief. It hadn't gone away, but he carried joy as well. He was no longer incapacitated. He would tell you he still suffers from the loss he experienced. He still feels very sad sometimes, and he always misses his son, but he would tell you that the depth of God's mercy met the depth of his pain. And he would also tell you that the experience of grief *and* joy has transformed him.

Samuel was in the fog of grief and disappointment when God approached him with a new assignment. God had plans for his kingdom and his prophet. Samuel's grief had become a stumbling block. He had to choose to let it go or at least not allow it to dominate him. He needed to finish his active mourning and resume his life. Maybe the new assignment would aid the process.

A fresh grief has hit our family. My twenty-two-year-old nephew (my husband's brother's son) was killed in a tragic event. We all have our theories as to why or how this could have happened, theories we seem to need, believing explanations will make us feel better. But the theories and explanations don't change the fact that this beautiful, inquisitive young man is gone.

At a communion service after his death, and with Julian on my mind, as I came forward I noticed the cross and remembered Jesus' mangled, lifeless body hanging on it. It was a sacrifice; it was also a statement, "I am really with you." The message of what happened to Jesus three days later is God's great gift to the world. If we embrace Jesus on the cross, if we see Jesus embracing us on the cross, he will raise us with him to glory. This hope does not take away terrible pain and grief that wrenches the heart and even the body, but it holds out a hope that the worst that can happen to us is not the final word.

A time comes to put away mourning clothes, to find a way through with God's help, to listen to God again for what is next, to let go of the crushing loss and sadness, or at least to put them in a place where they can't destroy us, to allow something new to co-exist with the grief, and to look to the future where, with God, there is always hope. Grief cannot be sidestepped, but God's question suggests that grief need not have the last word.

Prayer

Father,

I hold precious Julian up to you. I hold his parents before you and his sisters, too. Be with them every minute. Bring them through the terrible fog of grief. Give them the heart to bear their grief and show them how to allow joy to enter their hearts again too. Plan a glorious reunion.

You have always responded to my sadness with your compassion. It's not that missing someone goes away, or that every circumstance that caused me pain has been fixed to my liking. It is magical grace that transforms me and my life and makes me whole.

Thank you for the cross. I praise you for that.

Amen

Settle down in the presence of the Lord and meditate on this question "How long will you mourn?" Reflect about whatever comes to mind. Take time later to contemplate the questions in Further Reflections and the Bible verses below.

How long will you mourn?

Further Reflections

1. Draw a timeline. Below the line mark the major griefs you have experienced. Above the line, the most joyous experiences.

2. If you are grieving and God asked you how much longer will you grieve, what would your answer be? If you can't fathom a way out, listen for what God (or his agent) might say to you.

3. Is there one loss that has waylaid you? Can you open that dark place to God? Can you look for joy today?

Lectio Divina

Revelation 21:3-4
And I heard a loud voice from the throne saying, "Now the dwelling of God is with men, and he will live with them. They will be his people, and God himself will be with them and be their God. He will wipe every tear from their eyes. There will be no more death or mourning or crying or pain, for the old order of things has passed away."

Jeremiah 29:11
"For I know the plans I have for you," declares the Lord, "plans to prosper you and not to harm you. Plans to give you hope and a future."

Chapter 23

What are you doing here, Elijah?

The angel of the Lord came back a second time and touched him and said, "Get up and eat, for the journey is too much for you." So he got up and ate and drank. Strengthened by that food, he traveled forty days and forty nights until he reached Horeb, the mountain of God. There, he went into a cave and spent the night. And the word of the Lord came to him: "What are you doing here, Elijah?"

I Kings 19:7-9

Elijah the prophet had single-handedly defeated 450 prophets of Baal that King Ahab and his pagan wife Jezebel had installed in Israel. This spectacular showdown involved sacrifices and fire from heaven and the total impotence of Baal and his prophets, much to the humiliation of the evil Ahab and Jezebel. Through a number of miraculous feats, Elijah proved the Lord is the one true God, and then he killed the false prophets.

Jezebel and Ahab wanted him dead. Elijah was afraid and ran for his life, eventually all the way to Mt. Horeb, the mountain of God. There he hid in a cave. The Lord came to him and said, "What are you doing here, Elijah?" Elijah replied he has been zealous for the Lord, he was the only God-fearing man left in Israel, and now his life was on the line.

God did not try to reason or argue. Neither did he chastise him for his fear, nor even try to encourage him. Instead he told him to come out and watch because he, the Lord, would soon pass by. A violent storm blew in. It raged for hours. It shattered rocks and tore the mountain apart. The earth shook and a fire blazed.

You might think this fierce storm was the manifestation of God himself. But the account says God was not in the storm or the wind or the fire.

When the storm broke and it grew quiet, Elijah stood at the mouth of the cave and heard a whisper. This "still, small voice" was the manifestation. God had performed a private display just for Elijah. It was as if to say, "You think Jezebel and Ahab are in charge? I am."

Then the Lord asked him a second time, "What are you doing here, Elijah?"

Same question. I wonder if God emphasized different words: What are *you* doing here, Elijah? (You of all people know my power.) What are you are doing *here*, Elijah? (This is no time to run away.) What are you *doing* here, Elijah? (You have a calling; you have to go back.) I hear the question but then I hear something like this: "You are still my man. You are still my prophet: your mission is not yet over."

The gentle whisperer was trying to speak to something deep in Elijah, past the fear, the defensiveness, the depression. Elijah responded in the same way. "I've been zealous. I'm the only one left. They are trying to kill me." (That's why I'm hiding here in this cave.)

Elijah was renowned for his faith and his miracles. He had caused a three-year drought and then called forth the rain that ended the drought. He even brought a child back from the dead. But he ran from Ahab and Jezebel when they threatened to kill him. He ran, however, to the mountain of God, Mt. Horeb, also known as Mt. Sinai. This was where Moses and the elders met with the Lord and they, too, witnessed a storm, smoke, thunder, and fire. It was there that God gave Moses the Ten Commandments.

Elijah knew these stories. He ran to this mountain, into the very heart of it. When he was most vulnerable, most fearful, when he was threatened, he ran to the heart of God. You cannot run deep into the heart of God without running deep into your own heart at the same time. God met him there and in a quiet whisper asked him to tell him all about it.

This encounter with God was not about mighty wonders and miraculous feats, it was an encounter of intimacy. God again sought someone within his hiding place, to be with him, to encourage him and have a conversation with him.

Something similar also happened to David. He had powerful enemies and hid from them in a cave. Here's what he said in his hiding place:

> God, I'm crying out to you! I lift up my voice boldly to beg for your mercy.
> I spill out my heart to you and tell you all my troubles.
> For when I was desperate, overwhelmed, and about to give up,
> You were the only one there to help.
> You gave me a way of escape from the hidden traps of my enemies.
>
> *Psalm 142: 1-3* (The Passion Translation)

When have you been in Elijah's shoes? You've enjoyed a huge success. You've dazzled. God has done something big and grand and you played a big part. Then the next thing you know, fear has you on the run. Or perhaps the fear passes and that other old demon, depression, has you in lockdown. Or you face a threatening enemy and you are overwhelmed.

From time to time, during my quiet times with the Lord, I have found myself in a "cave." (This cave is not exactly a mystical vision; still it is more than my imagination.) The first time this happened, I think God was trying to get "me" out of the way. It felt like he had something in mind and he was concerned, in my impatience and anxiety, I might jump the gun and interfere with his agenda. My cave became a safe holding cell.

Other times, I felt like Elijah did and the cave was my hiding place from a perceived threat. It can be a comforting place to be.

Sometimes inhabiting the cave is the visual representation of the dark night of the soul.

Not too long ago, I found myself again inside the cave, and for the first time the cave opening was shut. I was sealed away. It was so dark, I could not see my hand in front of my face. But I sensed the presence of Jesus and heard him say he was with me and would never leave me. Again, I had the inkling that God was doing a work and I needed to bide my time.

Reflecting on this, I realized Elijah was not the only person who spent time in a cave. Jesus was laid in a tomb carved out of rock. When the stone was rolled over the entrance, it must have been pitch black inside as Jesus lay dead.

An ancient pattern is revealed here: In the beginning, when God created the world, he finished his work on the sixth day. Likewise, on Friday, the sixth day of the week, Jesus died on the cross and finished his work, too. In fact he proclaimed, "It is finished." On Saturday, the Sabbath, God rested and he blessed the day. Jesus also "rested" in his cave/tomb on the seventh day. On the first day of creation, God said, "Let there be light." On Sunday, the first day of the new week, the new era, Jesus, the light of the world, rose from the dead, leaving nothing but his shroud in the tomb.

Hiding in a cave, waiting for God, or even lying in a tomb, can be just the place God wants us to be. The cave can become a womb and resurrection life can spring forth. It is nothing we can do for ourselves. In the cave we wait with Elijah, with Jesus, for God to do his mysterious work.

God comes seeking us all, sinners and saints, "nobodies," and "somebodies." We call people who yearn for spiritual enlighten-ment and a deep connection to God "seekers," but God himself seems to be a seeker. He sought Elijah. Long before him, he sought Adam and Eve, Abraham and Sarah. He sought Jacob and Gideon, and the list goes on. He seeks us. Sometimes we look for signs and wonders and miss his subtle but persistence presence. We miss the whisper. We miss the conversation.

So what happened next to Elijah? He went back and continued his work for the Lord. Nobody killed him. Nobody even stopped him. And at the end of his life, he did not die a failure or afraid or defeated. He did not die at all. A fiery chariot picked him up and took him straight to heaven.

What kind of cave have you been in? When you find yourself in a cave, remember Elijah. In the quiet, listen for the whisper of God and what he might be asking you.

Prayer

Father,

Thank you for the times you have whispered in my heart. I often wish for unmistakable signs and miraculous wonders, but I truly treasure your quiet word.

I'm really sorry that I don't get quiet enough every day to hear you, even though what I have heard makes me yearn for more. Thank you for this grace.

And thank you for your plans for me, always for my welfare, always for your glory, always to make me an overcomer, too.

Amen

Again, settle down in the presence of the Lord and meditate on this question "What are you doing here?" Reflect about whatever comes to mind. Take time later to contemplate the questions in Further Reflections and the Bible verses below.

What are you doing here?

Further Reflections

1. Have you experienced a dark night or a season in a cave?

2. Is the idea of spending time alone in a cave appealing or terrifying to you? Would it offer you a welcome respite? Or would it feel like confinement or punishment?

3. Have you had a resurrection experience in your life? Do you need one now?

Lectio Divina

Isaiah 60:2
> See, darkness covers the earth,
> And thick darkness is over the peoples,
> But the Lord rises upon you
> And his glory appears over you.

John 11:38-39 & 41
> Jesus, once more deeply moved, came to the tomb. It was a cave with a stone laid across the entrance. "Take away the stone," he said...
> Jesus called in a loud voice, "Lazarus, come out!" The dead man came out, his hands and feet wrapped with strips of linen, and a cloth about his face.
> Jesus said to them, "Take off the grave clothes and let him go."

Chapter 24

Why do you disobey the Lord's commands?

Now Jehoiada [the priest] was old and full of years, and he died at the age of a hundred and thirty. He was buried with the kings in the City of David, because of the good he had done in Israel for God and his temple.

After the death of Jehoiada, the officials of Judah came and paid homage to the king, and he listened to them. They abandoned the temple of the Lord, the God of their fathers, and worshipped Asherah poles and idols. Because of their guilt, God's anger came upon Judah and Jerusalem. Although the Lord sent prophets to the people to bring them back to him, and though they testified against them, they would not listen.

Then the Spirit of God came upon Zechariah son of Jehoiada the priest. He stood before the temple and said, "This is what God says, 'Why do you disobey the Lord's commands? You will not prosper. Because you have forsaken the Lord, he has forsaken you'."

II Chronicles 24:15-20

This is the story of King Joash, who was a very good king of Judah for a long time—as long as the priest Jehoiada was alive. The two of them embarked on a project to restore and rebuild the temple from vandalism and atrocities that had occurred in years past. The people believed the temple was the very home of God, so this was holy work. Some years later, Jehoiada the priest died. He must have been the conscience of the king because, without his counsel, the king took a dark turn. Idol worshippers visited him, who talked the king into joining them at the pagan Asherah pole.

How did these "officials" do this? How did they get this king, who had been faithful for years, to abandon the Lord? And because he was the king, he led all the people to abandon the Lord, too.

First, the officials visited him and paid him homage. They complimented him, they bowed and scraped before him, and brought him gifts. Then they suggested the bright idea of Asherah poles where the people could worship other gods, worship that often included orgies with temple prostitutes. The account says, "He listened to them."

Maybe they said something like this: "We've seen some really amazing things. We've been to the Asherah poles! They are fantastic. We know a man as sophisticated as yourself would want to have one of his own. And the people love them too. You would become even more popular—even more powerful. The temple is… 'nice,' but Baal's temple is even more awesome. His temple has prostitutes! Doesn't that sound like fun! Be open.

You can be the cosmopolitan king. What's stopping you from including a few more gods and goddesses? You are the king, aren't you?"

Joash was enticed.

The prophet Zechariah confronted Joash about the idolatry. Zechariah was the son of the priest who had been so close to the king before he died. The king's new friends didn't like this, so they convinced Joash to kill Zechariah, and he had him stoned to death.

Not long after, a small army attacked Judah and King Joash was wounded. His own people then finished him off for what he had done to Zechariah. Some of the very people he had tried to please turned on Joash in the end.

This king started out strong in spirit and action. Instead of listening to the flattering officials, he could have heeded Zechariah when he came to speak the word of the Lord to him. He could have come to his senses.

Not only did he not listen, but he also silenced his own conscience and repressed any memory of kindness and affection for his old friend Jehoiada or for his son. How better to stop any nagging guilt about the course he had chosen? He killed the man who spoke God's question to him, "Why do you disobey?" in order to silence God himself.

"Why do you disobey?" was at least intended to check Joash, give him a time-out from his idol-worship, provide a time instead for self reflection and turning back to the truth. Joash refused the invitation, so the disobedience that began with the king listening to the wrong people, moved to idolatry, then murder, ultimately ending in his own death.

We might start to make or restore a home for God in our

own lives. Some of our friends or family or some people we want to impress may have other ideas. We listen. Before we know it, we are at the Asherah pole, too.

Only in our day, it probably won't look like a pagan worship service. It might not look idolatrous at all. But we abandon the temple, we abandon the Presence. We come up with myriad explanations and answers to the question of why we disobey, of why we no longer worship the Lord.

We can make excuses or we can instead look for the why. When were the seeds of disobedience planted? What made them so enticing? Was it greed? Lust? What was the pay off?

Sometimes we abandon God because we don't like the company he keeps. We may want more exotic enlightenment, something to set us apart from the crowd. We feel too sophisticated for quaint tradition. Or we have human passions we want to indulge and justify.

Maybe we don't take our disobedience as far as King Joash, and most of us don't influence a king anyway, however, we do have a sphere of influence and we may be unaware of the ripple effects of our own disobedience.

The final problem is that once we let Baal and Asherah into our lives, their influence can spread and they can be very difficult to expel.

We disobey God for lots of reasons. This question is designed to stop us in our tracks. Are we being influenced by the wrong people? Adam and Eve listened to the serpent. King Joash listened to "officials" who were probably making similar serpentine suggestions. It is a slippery slope from listening to indulgence to disobedience.

Prayer

Father,

Thank you for your written word. Thank you for truth that can free me from enticements to follow other "gods." More than any attachments I have on earth, or to people, places, and things, I want to be attached to you.

If I get off course, please send a prophet to me, too, and give me ears to hear!

Amen

Settle down in the presence of the Lord and meditate on this question, "Why do you disobey the Lord' commands?" Reflect about whatever comes to mind. Take time later to contemplate the questions in Further Reflections and the Bible verses below.

Why do you disobey the Lord's commands?

Further Reflections

1. When have you been persuaded to participate in something contrary to your beliefs in spite of your own conscience?

2. What stand (stands) have you taken for what you believe?

Lectio Divina

Deuteronomy 18: 14-15
   The nations you will dispossess listen to those who practice sorcery or divination. But as for you, the Lord your God has not permitted you to do so. The Lord your God will raise up for you a prophet like me from among your own brothers. You must listen to him.

1 John 3:21-24
   Dear friends, if our hearts do not condemn us, we have confidence before God and receive from him anything we ask, because we obey his commands and do what pleases him. And this is his command: to believe in the name of his Son, Jesus Christ, and to love one another as he commanded us. Those who obey his commands live in him, and he in them. And this is how we know that he is in us: We know it by the Spirit he gave us.

Chapter 25

Where were you when I laid the earth's foundation?

Then the Lord answered Job out of the storm. He said: "Who is this that darkens my counsel with words without knowledge? Brace yourself like a man; I will question you and you will answer me. Where were you when I laid the earth's foundations?"

Job 38:2-4

The story of Job unfolds like a play. In the opening scene, we learn Job was an excellent man; he was wealthy, good, and noble. He had a family he loved and he honored God. In the next scene, God was in the company of angels in the heavenly realm, but Satan also was present. God was so proud of Job that he bragged about him. "There is no one on earth like him; he is blameless and upright, a man who fears God and shuns evil." (*Job 1:8*).

Satan, the accuser, stood ready with an accusation. He suggested to God that Job's faith and moral character were merely the result of his wealth, along with his happy and healthy family. In other words, Job was good because he had good things; he had faith only because he was blessed. Take those things away and Job would surely lose faith and curse God.

God and Satan then made a wager and God bet on Job. Satan was sure he could get Job to reject his faith. He set about destroying his livestock, his servants and children, and in the end, Satan attacked Job himself. After all these assaults, the Bible says, "Job did not sin by charging God with wrongdoing." (*Job 1:22*). Satan even upped the ante and caused more suffering, but again, "Job did not sin in what he said." (Job 2:10).

In the next act, Job's close friends visited him to commiserate about all of his misfortunes. They were convinced that all that happened must somehow be Job's fault, that he must have committed some serious crime or sin that would explain his "punishment." They advised him to search his conscience and repent of *something*.

Of course, we know Job wasn't being punished at all, but *they* didn't know that and maintained that Job wouldn't be suffering like this unless he deserved it. Job argued with them because he knew he hadn't done anything to deserve the catastrophes befalling him. He didn't curse God (which was Satan's prediction and his wife's suggestion), but he did begin to question *why*.

With no knowledge of the back story, Job and his friends crafted theological sounding arguments trying to convince each other of their "truth." The theological discussions, debates, and arguments went back and forth for days. Another friend then joined the debate and summed up the opposing sides:

1. Job's friends, attempting to maintain that God is just, condemned Job of guilt with no evidence except the apparent consequences of his sin.
2. Job maintained his innocence but questioned *why*, even *demanding* to know why.

At this impasse, the final act occured; God himself arrived on the scene. He did not address the dispute between Job and his friends nor did he bother to defend himself. He didn't explain the conversation with Satan which had set the whole chain of events in motion. He never told any of them why. Rather, he asked questions, beginning with these two, "Who is this that darkens my counsel with words without knowledge?" and "Where were you when I laid the earth's foundation?"

The inquiry continued: "Have you ever given orders to the morning, or shown the dawn its place? Have you journeyed to the springs of the sea or walked in the recesses of the deep? Have you comprehended the vast expanses of the earth? What is the way to the abode of light? And where does darkness reside? Can you bring forth the constellations in their seasons? Do you know the layers of heaven? Who endowed the heart with wisdom or gave understanding to the mind? Who provides food for the raven when its young cry out to God and wander about for lack of food?" (*Job 38*).

On one hand, the questions themselves were a gentle reprimand to Job and his friends. They highlighted two things. Their answer to all these questions would have to be, "We don't know," thus suggesting just how *much* they don't know.

At the same time, the questions pointed out that God *does* know all these things, suggesting some things remain a mystery to us, but not to him. To assign reasons for things not fully understood can result in very wrong conclusions. Human logic applied to incomplete facts will not produce trustworthy explanations. Secondly, the questions highlighted that we are sometimes mistaken about what we really *need* to know. Instead of looking for an explanation or devising a systematic, rational theology, maybe what we most need is a revelation of God.

The questions paint a poetic and evocative picture of creation. God created all things; he sustains his creation; nothing is beyond him, not the Milky Way, not the galaxies, nor our earth. Not the birth of mountain goats, the well-being of wild donkeys, the joy of the ostrich, the strength and beauty of the horse, or the flight of the hawk. (*Job 39*). The entire speech is a shimmering description of our breathtaking world. God delights in it all and he invited Job to delight in it, too. It is all good. It's as though God said, "Look at my universe, Job. Isn't it magnificent? You don't know how I created it, there is much you don't understand, but behold the glory!"

You might think Job wouldn't be satisfied with this response from God because it didn't address his personal situation; God never gave an explanation. Yet Job was astounded. He seemed to remember that in spite of his terrible circumstances, God is good. God is strong. He has the last word.

God's questions to Job reframed his perspective. They were an invitation to him to lift his eyes off his problems, to look at the one who loves him and holds all the answers. For a long time, all Job could see was his own misfortune. God's questions shifted his attention; he saw God's creation with fresh eyes, and in that he somehow saw God afresh, too. It was enough for him.

In fact, it was such a magnificent revelation, such an expansive picture of the greatness of God, that Job was practically speechless. "I am unworthy—how can I reply to you? I put my hand over my mouth" (*Job 40:4*).

Beholding creation, noticing its beauty, and realizing God made it all can bring us wisdom that theological questions and answers cannot touch. God's soliloquy reminded Job of the enchantment of the universe. It also reminded him that the one who created it all, who says he is on our side (in spite of any "evidence" to the contrary), can be trusted.

Most of us, or at least many of us, stand in Job's shoes at some time in our lives. Just by being human, we are at risk for incredible loss. When we anticipate it, we think it will destroy us and we do anything or believe anything in an attempt to ward it off. If it comes out of the blue, we are devastated. "My God, why did you let this happen? You could have stopped it! Why did you do this to me? Why have you abandoned me?" That's the cry of our hearts.

It was also Jesus' cry from the cross. He participated in the universal human anguish, and he told us he only does what he sees the father doing (*John 5:19*). God joins us in our suffering, whether we are aware of his presence (and his suffering) or not.

Many people stop believing in God or turn to active resentment of him due to the tragedies on the planet or because of their own personal suffering. They say: "If there is a God, then why does he allow so much suffering? Why did he let this happen to me? If he exists at all, I want nothing to do with him." They don't know the whole story.

The book of Job is a template for those of us who have ever suffered and asked God, "Why?" Bad things happen to good people; we don't know why. God asks us to believe in his goodness anyway. We have an enemy we cannot see who accuses us and attempts to deceive, seduce, and destroy us. We are not told all the reasons why. This enemy tries to convince us that the bad things that happen mean God doesn't care, doesn't love us, or is not very powerful after all. He further insinuates that we are only getting what we deserve, so why would God help us anyway? This enemy tells us there is no such thing as grace. Even our friends' compassion is tinged with a critique of where we must have gone wrong.

Some readers today join the chorus of analysts by citing this verse: "What I feared has come upon me; what I dreaded has happened to me." (*Job 3:25*). They surmise Job's prior fear was the real loophole Satan used as an opening to attack this good man. Maybe they're onto something, but the whole story of Job seems to be a cautionary tale, a warning, that when we analyze what God is doing and why, we often have "words without knowledge."

When God sent his own son as one of us, the same enemy who tried to ruin Job did everything he could to destroy God's son. And for three days it looked like he succeeded. The great creator God, whom Job glimpsed, has the final word after all. And in the story of his son, we are told why: "For God so loved the world" (*John 3:16*).

We may never stop asking God why, but he may often not answer us. If you are wrestling with a 'why' question of your own that hasn't been answered, try reading all the questions God asks Job in chapters 38 and 39. Put your own question on the back burner. Soak yourself either literally or imaginatively in the beauty of nature, then listen to what God might be asking you

Prayer

Lord,

Please forgive me for all the misguided theologies I have adopted to explain the things I don't understand. Please help me to trust you when misfortune befalls me, and please tell me what to do. I love the questions you asked Job, the magnificent portrait of your creation. I love your creation, too.

I remember the line from the poem by Edna St. Vincent Millay, "Oh world, I cannot hold thee close enough." I sing that line in my heart when I am stopped in my tracks by the beauty of this earth. I sing praise and gratitude in my heart to you. I proclaim, "Bravo!"

This beauty dazzles. It is an awesome revelation.

Amen

Settle down in the presence of the Lord and meditate on this question, "Where were you when I laid the earth's foundation?" Reflect about whatever comes to mind. Take time later to contemplate the questions in Further Reflections and the Bible verses below.

Where were you when I laid the earth's foundation?

Further Reflections

1. Have you asked God a "why" question? If so, has it been answered or is it still open? How has it affected your beliefs, your trust and love of God?

2. What in creation elicits awe in you? How has the beauty of creation healed you, sustained you or blessed you?

Lectio Divina

Genesis 1:31
    God saw all that he had made, and it was very good.

Proverbs 8:27-31(The Message Translation)
    I was there when he set the heavens in place,
    when he marked out the horizon on the face of the deep,
    when he established the clouds above,
    when he gave the sea its boundaries so the waters would
    not overstep his command,
    and when he marked out the foundations of the earth.
    Then I was the craftsman at his side.
    I was filled with delight day after day, rejoicing in his
    presence,
    rejoicing in his whole world and delighting in mankind.

Chapter 26

Would you condemn me to justify yourself?

Brace yourself like a man; I will question you, and you shall answer me. Would you discredit my justice? Would you condemn me to justify yourself?

Job 40:7-8

As we've already seen, the book of Job deals with our insatiable demand to know why bad things happen. Philosophers and theologians have tackled this issue and drawn elaborate and often competing ideas in their attempt to craft an answer. God doesn't explain himself or answer Job or his friends, he just keeps asking Job questions.

His final two:

1. "Would you discredit my justice?" (Job, would you lay at my feet what Satan has done and then determine that I am unjust?), and

2. "Would you condemn me to justify yourself?" (You assume that when bad things happen there's got to be a reason, and you so want to be justified that you're willing to blame me?)

We regard our circumstances around two fundamental principles: we want to know why, and we want to know who's to blame. If something bad happens, *somebody* has to get the blame. It better not be me.

This is the first time God has raised these questions about blame, but we've seen them coming. In the first pages of Genesis, when God confronted Adam about the forbidden fruit, Adam said, "The woman you gave me, she made me eat it."

So it's Eve's fault, but apparently God's fault, too. He was the one who "gave" her to him after all. We nurse grievances, we lose friendships, marriages founder, partnerships fail, all because we so desperately want to justify ourselves. We condemn others, but we don't stop there. When we blame others, we are, in essence, blaming God. Behind the blame is always the suggestion that God caused it—or, at least, allowed it—so really it's his fault. The lie creeps in. *God is withholding from me. He is not really for me. He doesn't care. He is not to be trusted. He's not real anyway.*

When we complain about our lot in life, give in to envy, rail about our circumstances or the many injustices we have endured, or when we just lack gratitude in our hearts, we are in reality blaming God. We would rather justify ourselves at all costs, even if it condemns him.

In the case at hand, the whole goal of Satan was to get Job to curse God. He did not succeed. After the first round of destruction, we learn, "In all this, Job did not sin by charging God with wrongdoing" (*Job 1:22*).

There's one more thing Job never did. He never described what happened to him—everything (we know) that *Satan* did—as "God's will" and thereby slander God's character.

Maybe this is why in the end God said to Job's friend, "I am angry with you and your two friends, [the ones who had "consoled" Job] because you have not spoken of me what is right, as my servant Job has" (*Job 42:7*).

After God asked these questions, he described two beasts: the behemoth and the leviathan. No man could capture, subdue, or control either.

The message: Danger lurks in this world, inducing fear, and we concoct many schemes to control it. God leaves it a mystery.

However if we are attacked by a fierce wild beast on land or at sea, the behemoth or the leviathan, and we blame God, we may need to reassess. We cut ourselves off from the only one who can control the behemoth and the leviathan. We would also be cutting ourselves off from the comfort and wisdom of

God.

If we suffer like Job, and fall for Satan's ploy to renounce God, we are still left with our problem and our suffering. They don't go away just because we dispense with God.

At some time in our lives, many of us, even the most long suffering and faithful, pray two prayers:

1. "Oh God, please don't let this happen," and
2. "Oh, God, *why* did you let this happen?"

They are legitimate prayers. God answers them sometimes, but sometimes, like Job, bad thing happens and we will never know why.

Job was humbled. He said to God, "I know that you can do all things; no plan of yours can be thwarted... Surely I spoke of things I did not understand, things too wonderful for me to know... My ears had heard of you but now my eyes have seen you" (*Job 40: 2* & *5*).

God's questions and the continuing revelation changed everything for Job, even without any concrete answer to his "why" question. Before this encounter, he knew *about* God, he even worshipped him, now he knows him. Asking "why" was a dead end. In truth, what Job needed was a revelation. He needed more than hearing *about* God, and he certainly needed more than the ideas, programs and the analysis offered by his friends. Philosophy is cold comfort when we are bereft.

Like Job, we sometimes need a direct experience of God. In the middle of a tragedy or in its aftermath, we need to *see* God or *hear* his voice, and most of all to realize he loves us and will never abandon us, nor will he abandon what we entrust to him. Or perhaps we find ourselves in the position of his misguided friends, so sure we know the reasons why. We are like children who shut our eyes, cover our ears, and just keep talking. We end up missing God when he does show up.

Before the curtain falls, God instructed Job to pray for his friends, the ones who had been so insistent in their diagnosis of the situation, who believed Job's sin opened the door to all his calamities, the ones who had been completely wrong about Job and about God. Even so, God wanted them restored, too. And in the end, after he had prayed for his friends, God blessed Job again. He blessed the latter part of his life much more than the first, because it always seems to be God's nature to bless.

The message of Job is that in our ignorance we can contrive elaborate reasons for things we don't understand. We can blame others when they are not at fault. We are tempted to ascribe evil to God, even though he is not the enemy.

God is always good, he is still for us, ever worthy to be trusted. Even when we get it all wrong, he is "for" us, and he loves us immensely, despite any disasters, symptoms, losses, or tragedies we may experience, or the circumstances we find ourselves in. Our circumstances are a faulty barometer of God's love and favor.

Prayer

Lord,

I believe you are really good—but this life can be so hard. I very often look for a way to have some kind of control, sometimes even trying to control you. You challenge me to trust you and live with joy and courage even when I'm scared, even when bad things happen and especially when I don't understand.

You are the one who created the sun, the moon, and all the stars. You take care of mountain goats, wild donkeys, ostriches, horses, and hawks. You can take care of me, too.

Thank you.

Amen

Settle down in the presence of the Lord and meditate on this question, "Would you condemn me to justify yourself?" Reflect about whatever comes to mind. Take time later to contemplate the questions in Further Reflections and the Bible verses below.

Would you condemn me to justify yourself?

Further Reflections

1. Do you suppose that you harbor distrust of God (if you do) because you have believed that he is the author of your suffering?

2. Ask God to reveal who he really is and what is in his heart for you. Write down what you "hear."

Lectio Divina

Genesis 3:12-13
    The man said, "The woman you put here with me—she gave me some fruit from the tree, and I ate it." Then the Lord said to the woman, "What is this you have done?" The woman said, "The serpent deceived me, and I ate it."

Psalm 119:68 (Living Bible)
    You are good and do only good; make me follow your lead.

PART 5

THE PROPHETS
GOD SPEAKS TO
HIS NATION

Chapters 27 - 34

Once the nation of Israel was established, the people enjoyed years of peace and prosperity, but soon enough some political and religious rulers became corrupt, many of them instituting idol worship. Often, one exploitive king followed one good king. The fate of the nation waxed and waned, depending on who was in power. God called, however, a number of people—the prophets—to speak boldly to the leaders and the people and to confront them when necessary. Contrary to what their title suggests, their message was not limited to forecasting the future, though they did make predictions.

For example, Nathan was a prophet during the reign of David. Nathan confronted him about committing adultery with Bathsheba and elicited his repentance. Joel, another prophet, foretold that David would have a descendent (the messiah) whose reign would never end. Joel also foretold that one day the gift of prophecy would be poured out on all God's people. The best kings listened to the prophets and heeded their words.

The prophets became God's confidantes and served as his messengers, even as critics, to the political, economic, and religious rulers. The prophets also often had mystical encounters with God. They developed fierce faith. They needed it; they often had to speak uncomfortable truth to those in power. They were the voice of God to generations of people.

Years later Peter quoted Joel's ancient prediction to explain the dramatic day of Pentecost when the Holy Spirit came upon believers praying together after Jesus' death and resurrection: "In the last days," God says, "I will pour out my Spirit on all people. Your sons and daughters will prophesy, your young men will see visions and your old men will dream dreams" (*Acts 2:17*). God intended all along to pour out his Spirit and be in close relationship to all of us, to communicate with us in all kinds of ways, to be on intimate terms with us all. He intended for his people—*all his people*—to be his spokesmen and women.

The questions in this section are questions God posed to the prophets or to his people through the prophets. Before you begin these questions, pause and reflect on these words: "prophecy," "calling," and "destiny." Think about times when someone spoke truth or encouragement to you, or about times when you were the one God called to share his truth with someone else.

Chapter 27

What more could have been done for my vineyard than I have done for it? When I looked for good grapes, why did it yield only bad?

"Now you dwellers in Jerusalem and men of Judah, judge between me and my vineyard. What more could have been done for my vineyard than I have done for it? When I looked for good grapes, why did it yield only bad?"

Isaiah 5:3-4

God loves gardens. Eden was the lovely garden God prepared for his first family. The Promised Land was the new "garden" for the family of Abraham. Joshua and Caleb later described it as a land flowing with milk and honey. Beauty, nature, fertile soil, shade trees, fruit trees, river beds, and waterfalls were all included in the home he prepared for his children. The whole planet was to be the garden home of mankind.

Early in the ministry of Isaiah, God spoke of this theme in a story called *The Song of the Vineyard*. It started as a beautiful parable of God and his people. In the story, the vineyard owner created a vineyard on a fertile hill. He cleared the land, planted the best vines, and built a watchtower and a wine press. He thought it was lovely. God then explained, "The vineyard of the Lord Almighty is the house of Israel and the men of Judah are his garden of delight" (*Isaiah 5:7a*).

There was just one problem: the vineyard yielded only bad grapes.

According to the metaphor, just as a vineyard is to yield a harvest of good fruit, so, too, Israel was to produce good fruit, fruit of faithfulness, holiness, justice, righteousness, peace, and love. Instead it kept sliding into idolatry and disobedience. Over and over God rescued the Israelites from their enemies, disciplined them, called them to faith, and loved them, but their faithfulness in return never lasted for long. In frustration God said to Isaiah, "What more could I have done?"

The question is reminiscent of a friend baring her anguish

about her wayward child. "I love him so much. I've given him every advantage, but he sabotages his life at every turn and now he wants nothing to do with me. What more could I have done?"

Or it's suggestive of a solemn doctor informing the family, "We've done all we can. I'm afraid it doesn't look good."

Isaiah doesn't answer.

There was really no answer to this question. It hung in the air, and then God posed the follow-up question, "Why did the vineyard yield only bad grapes?"

His questions became an indictment against the people. They also indicated a connection between what God had done for Israel and what he could therefore expect in return. These questions raise the further issue of what counts as good or bad fruit.

Isaiah contrasted the particular fruit God looked for with what he saw: "And he looked for justice and saw bloodshed; for righteousness, but heard cries of distress" (*Isaiah 5:7b*). Bloodshed and distress would qualify as bad fruit.

It was time for judgment. Isaiah predicted the Assyrians would attack Israel sooner or later, and God would not intervene to save them. Years later the Babylonians attacked Judah, and God did not rescue them either.

The story of God and his people, however, did not end with defeat. Over the course of Isaiah's life and ministry, God answered his question, "What more could I have done?" by revealing to Isaiah what more he would do.

God would initiate a new covenant. He promised a new kingdom: a baby will be born, and a drama will take place in another garden (*Isaiah 9* and *53*). The long-ago blessing promised to Abraham and Sarah, and before them to Adam and

Eve, will be poured out for everyone. In spite of their bad fruit, God had a good plan in store for anyone who believed him and received his gift. He unfolded a plan of redemption, not just for Israel but for the whole world.

God's question about bad fruit is relevant for us today. The analogous question for each of us: what has God done for *me* and what am I producing?

People can produce two kinds of fruit. First is an interior fruit of the soul. Paul enumerates the fruit that comes from being filled with the Holy Spirit: "love, joy, peace, patience, kindness, goodness, faithfulness, gentleness, and self-control" (*Galatians 5:22*).

Next is the outer manifestation of this fruit, actions that demonstrate to others, on small or grand scales and in myriad ways, the manifestation of these inner qualities.

Jesus has much to say about this. I point out two things here:

1. There is only one way to bear lasting fruit (inner and outer fruit).

   "Remain in me, and I will remain in you. No branch can bear fruit by itself; it must remain in the vine. Neither can you bear fruit unless you remain in me. I am the vine; you are the branches. If a man remains in me and I in him, he will bear much fruit; apart from me you can do nothing."

   (*John 15: 4-5*).

And 2. He gives an explanation of bad fruit.

"The kingdom of heaven is like a man who sowed
good seed in his field. But while everyone was sleeping,
his enemy came and sowed weeds among the wheat,
and went away. When the wheat sprouted and formed
heads, then the weeds also appeared. The owner's
servants came to him and said, 'Sir, didn't you sow
good seed in your field? Where then did the weeds
come from?' 'An enemy did this,' he replied."

(Matthew 13: 24-28)

If you see God's gifts to you, but at the same time bad fruit
is in your life, (mangled relationships, a derailed career, over-
reliance on alcohol, anger, selfishness, depression, or anxiety),
then it might be a good idea to look at the seeds of this bad
fruit. Has the enemy planted weeds in your life? Perhaps you
are working hard to produce good things all by yourself apart
from Jesus and the Holy Spirit. Perhaps, like the Israelites, other
"gods" enticed you, other "gods" who promised just the lifestyle
you want, or who fit in better with the company you keep.

It might be time to cultivate the soil of your heart. Take a
look at your worries and anxieties which can choke the life of
any good seed. It might also be important to remember that
God did not give up on his people or his plan, so he has not
given up on you either. He continues to have blessings in store
for you and good plans for your life.

The questions suggest that God had already provided everything his people needed to live a happy and productive life,
so perhaps he has provided all I need as well. My feelings of
neediness can blind me to what is already available. In fact, the
sense that I need one more thing, (and there is *always* one more

thing), can become a bad habit. Looking over my shoulder at what my neighbor has can makes me dismissive about what I have.

Maybe I'm looking in the wrong direction. The new covenant of faith and the Holy Spirit are available to everyone through the son he sent to redeem us all. I can miss out on what I already possess because I don't see the giver or the gifts clearly enough.

Prayer

Father,

The story of the vineyard reminds me of the beauty of your world. When I see even a humble row or two of vines planted in a neighbor's yard, it speaks of your love and care, calling me back to the noble task of allowing you and cooperating with you, to plant, weed, prune, water, and harvest in my life.

Each day I choose, at least for a little while, to bask in the warmth of your sacred garden.

Amen

Settle down in the presence of the Lord and meditate on this question, "What more could have been done for my vineyard than I have done for it? When I looked for good grapes, why did it yield only bad?" Reflect about whatever comes to mind. Take time later to contemplate the questions in Further Reflections and the Bible verses below.

What more could I do?
When I look for good grapes,
why do I find only bad?

Further Reflections

1. Make a list of the bad fruit and the good fruit in your life.

2. In what ways could you tend to the soil of your heart or your relationship to God that might make a difference in your "fruit"?

Lectio Divina

Isaiah 61:11
> For as the soil makes the sprout come up
> and a garden causes seeds to grow,
> so the Sovereign Lord will make
> righteousness and praise
> spring up before all nations.

Jeremiah 17:7-8
> "But blessed is the man who trusts in the Lord,
> whose confidence is in him.
> He will be like a tree planted by the water
> that sends out its roots by the stream.
> It does not fear when heat comes;
> its leaves are always green.
> It has no worries in a year of drought
> and never fails to bear fruit."

Chapter 28

Whom shall I send?
And who will go for us?

"Woe to me!" I cried. "I am ruined! For I am a man of unclean lips, and I live among a people of unclean lips, and my eyes have seen the King, the Lord Almighty."

Then one of the seraphs flew to me with a live coal in his hand, which he had taken with tongs from the altar. With it he touched my mouth and said, "See, this has touched your lips; your guilt is taken away and your sin atoned for."

Then I heard the voice of the Lord saying, "Whom shall I send? And who will go for us?"

Isaiah 6:5-8

At the beginning of his book, Isaiah told the story of the vineyard and then he recounted how he came to be a prophet. He had an amazing vision. It was his "burning bush" moment, his calling by God, and it was very dramatic. He beheld a vision of the heavenly temple.

Isaiah saw God sitting on a throne. His train was magnificent. Angels worshipped him and called to each other, "Holy, holy, holy is the Lord Almighty; the whole earth is full of his glory" (*Isaiah 6:3*). The temple was filled with smoke, and the doorposts shook. Isaiah was awestruck, but the vision also made him anxious because in this holy presence he was aware of how unholy and unclean he was. He was afraid of being struck down on the spot. Then one of the angels brought a live coal from the altar, touched it to his lips, and pronounced forgiveness and atonement.

In the next scene, God said, "Whom shall I send? And who will go for us?"

It was as though Isaiah listened in on a holy conversation. The voice must have reverberated in heaven. To this open-ended question Isaiah said, "Here am I. Send me."

Compare Isaiah's response with some of the others who were called by God. He didn't tell God why he was not the right guy or why it wouldn't work. He didn't argue or beg him to find someone else. Right away he said he would go, though he didn't even know yet where he was to go or what he was to do. He was told it wasn't going to be easy. God informed Isaiah that the people would not listen to him, nor would they heed his warnings or take his prophecies to heart. They would continue in their stubborn, selfish rebellion—even though, as God told Isaiah, they could turn at any time and be healed (Isaiah 6:10).

Perhaps Isaiah said "yes" because he was overwhelmed by such a majestic vision. Perhaps it's easier to argue with the Lord (as Moses did) when he comes incognito as a burning bush, or (as Gideon did) when he who shows up in a winepress, or in a dusty tent, or as a mysterious stranger in the middle of the night. It is easier to dismiss God's call when it's presented as a subtle prompting. Isaiah could have remained silent.

The question was not an order or even a request. It wasn't clear from the question what the mission would even be. Would you say "yes" before you knew the terms?

As it turned out, this was not a one-time mission. The assignment would last through at least four kingships, the destruction of the northern kingdom at the hands of the Assyrians, and prophetically looking years ahead to the Babylonian captivity of Judah. By Isaiah's time, Israel and Judah had split into two kingdoms, and they both were sliding into idolatry and immorality. Isaiah preached and warned and prophesied. Ever faithful, he delivered the messages from God. It didn't seem to have any effect. Isaiah also reported many promises from God that he would never live to see fulfilled. He would never know the outcome.

I found myself in such a situation a few years ago. I was dealing with a sticky situation that I couldn't fix, God was not rushing in to save the day, and I had no idea what the outcome would be. Then I had a dream. In the dream, Jesus stood before me and a voice said, "The reason Jesus was such a man of peace is that he knew the outcome was not up to him." The idea was that he lived in complete reliance upon the Father. For me this was not a theological statement, it was a personal message that I desperately needed to hear. Here's why.

My common response to any problem is believing "It's all up to me." This causes me much stress, but regardless of the stress, I'm reluctant to change my ways. If the solution is up to me, I can attempt to craft the solution I want. Entrusting it to God means surrendering that sense of control. Before my dream, I had no peace. I did not trust him with the situation. I had not surrendered to him the outcome I wanted, and I was leery of how and what he might do.

Hearing from God in the dream gave me the courage to entrust it all to him. Three weeks later I saw the first signs of a breakthrough.

Sometime after this encounter with God, I came across a passage in the book of Daniel, a prophet who followed years after Isaiah. Daniel also had visions, dreams, and wondrous experiences with God and his angels. He was told mysterious things that he didn't always understand. He, too, wanted to know the outcome.

> I heard, but I did not understand. So I said, "My Lord, what will the outcome of all this be?"
> He replied, "Go your way, Daniel, because the words are closed up and sealed until the time of the end."
> (*Daniel 12:8-9*)

Often the outcomes are not up to us, and many things remain shrouded in mystery. Our job is to show up, either physically or spiritually or both. We have to muster the faith we possess or seek at least a mustard seed of faith. We have to reject the fear and the lies that fear engenders. Sometimes we might have a specific task to perform, and we need to be obedient.

Sometimes we have to "go our way." We have responsibilities and accountability, but if we entrust a matter to God, then the outcome is up to him. Likewise, even when he entrusts a matter to us, the ultimate outcome is up to him.

Isaiah had a lifetime call, and God's prediction about how the people would receive him proved true. They didn't listen to him. They continued in their idolatry. He did not bring about any sustained breakthroughs in the people. But Isaiah must have known or learned the same truth God told me. The outcome was not up to him; and though he didn't live to see all that God told him, he served God for the rest of his life. Through him, wonderful promises were given that came to pass centuries after Isaiah spoke them.

Some of us doubt we have a calling or a destiny, or we're not sure what it is. It may be that God says again and again, "Whom can we send? Who will go for us?" We may find ourselves in dangerous territory and not realize that God's strategy has placed us there to do a job he singled us out to do. Our job may be to pray for *his* outcome.

Perhaps wrapped up in our destiny is not just how well we perform our work or how successful the world deems us to be, but how we come to deal with situations that seem impossible and learn to trust the one who calls. Our destiny is discovered not just by what we create but by becoming men and women of great love and peace and joy; the people God created us to be. Our destiny is in our relationship with the God who calls.

A "call" from God is really an invitation. Chances are you will get more than one opportunity to say "yes" to God's invitation. But you never know what happy venture or what challenging task or life-changing encounter might pass you by if you say "no thanks" too many times.

Prayer

Lord,

I don't know what you have in store for me next, but please show me what I can do for you now, or what you want me to be or learn to be. Please make me ready for you and your work and whatever lies ahead. Give me a heart that says "yes" to you and a willingness to do whatever you want.

In the meantime, I say a joyful "yes" to you right now.

Amen

Settle down in the presence of the Lord and meditate on this question, "Whom shall I send? Who will go for us?" Reflect about whatever comes to mind. Take time later to contemplate the questions in Further Reflections and the Bible verses below.

Whom shall I send?
Who will go for us?

Further Reflections

1. Do you want to be caught up into a grand purpose or mission, or truthfully do you have enough on your plate right now? Do you sense that your life, as it is right now, is actually a grand mission?

2. What call from God might be in front of you that you have not recognized? Does it seem you've miss the call?

Lectio Divina

Genesis 12:1-4a
    The Lord had said to Abraham, "Leave your country, your people, and your father's household and go to a land I will show you..." So Abraham left.

Exodus 3:4
    God called to him from within the bush, 'Moses, Moses!" And Moses said, "Here I am."

I Samuel 3:7-10
    Now Samuel did not yet know the Lord. The word of the Lord had not yet been revealed to him.

The Lord called Samuel a third time and Samuel got up and went to Eli and said, "Here I am; you called me."

Then Eli realized that the Lord was calling the boy. So Eli told Samuel, "Go and lie down, and if he calls you, say, "Speak, Lord, for your servant is listening." So Samuel went and lay down in his place.

The Lord came and stood there, calling as at the other times, "Samuel! Samuel!"

Then Samuel said, "Speak, for your servant is listening."

Chapter 29

Does the clay say to the potter, "What are you making?"

Woe to him who quarrels with his maker, to him who is but a potsherd among the potsherds on the ground. Does the clay say to the potter, "What are you making?"

Isaiah 45:9

For years Isaiah had warned the Israelites about a looming catastrophic defeat if they did not repent and reform their ways. The Assyrians had already destroyed the northern kingdom. Then Isaiah looked to the future and to what would become of Judah. It, too, would be defeated, it would look like the end, but the captivity would be temporary. God had a plan for their salvation.

What was surprising was the one God had chosen to be their savior. He announced in advance that he would choose Cyrus, the foreign ruler of Persia, to deliver the Israelites from Babylon. Some of his people objected. Their attitude was that Cyrus (a pagan gentile) was the last person God should enlist to save his people.

Hence the question, "Does the clay say to the potter, "What are you making?" God made the point: he is sovereign, whom he chooses and for what purpose is his decision.

We're not told very much about Cyrus and the role he played, but a brief account appears in II Chronicles. Long before Cyrus showed up, the Babylonians had not only conquered Judah, they had burned the temple, broken down the walls of Jerusalem, and taken many as slaves back to Babylon. You could say that just as the temple was broken to pieces, the Israelites were also decimated; they were mere "potsherds" in a foreign land.

Their captivity lasted several decades; then the nation of Persia defeated Babylon, and the King of Persia acquired the Israelite captives. And then:

> In the first year of Cyrus King of Persia, in order to fulfill the word of the Lord spoken to Jeremiah, the Lord moved the heart of Cyrus King of Persia to make a proclamation throughout the realm and to put it in writing:
> This is what Cyrus king of Persia says: "The Lord, the God of heaven, has given me all the kingdoms of the earth and he has appointed me to build a temple for him at Jerusalem in Judah. Anyone of his people among you—may the Lord his God be with him, and let him go up."
>
> (*II Chronicles 36: 22-23*)

Any of the Jewish captives who wanted to could go home. Surely Cyrus had his own reasons for setting them free. Maybe diplomatic or political strategies motivated him. But the reason behind those reasons was that "the Lord moved the heart of Cyrus king of Persia." According to the metaphor, God is the potter and he decides whom he will choose to work with and through.

You would think there must have been an easier way for God to accomplish the deliverance of his people and the eventual reestablishment of the kingdom of Judah. After all, it took a war between Persia and Babylon before Cyrus could even be in a position of authority and power. Was there not anyone on the scene already who was available to deliverer the captives? Was there not some contemporary Moses or Joshua who could do it? Any Israelite would be preferable.

God often uses surprising people in surprising ways to

accomplish his ends. His question, "Does the clay say to the potter, 'What are you making?'" suggests some didn't (and still don't) approve of his methods. It is all too easy for us to think we know what God will and will not do, whom he will and will not use, and what his agenda is. It is all too easy to jump next to what we think God *should* do and whom he *should* pick to do it, and then harbor critical thoughts about the potter when he doesn't comply with our ideas.

Sometimes we do comprehend what the potter is up to, but other times we should be more prudent in our conjectures and judgments. No doubt we have all questioned the potter's tactics when he has chosen someone not of our ilk—not of our tribe—for an important task. The Cyrus episode was a signpost to something that would happen hundreds of year later. When Jesus began his ministry, the religious establishment was aghast that this backwater Galilean would or could be God's chosen one.

Here is an additional way to think about the metaphor of the potter and the clay. Who is God creating me to be and how do I feel about that? God is speaking directly to me. I'm the clay on the wheel. How much or how little am I cooperating with him? Am I even paying attention when God moves my heart? Am I malleable like clay or do I resist with every turn of the wheel?

The truth is that I can get suspicious about what God is up to. Before I see the finished product, I may think he's making one mistake after another. Or I may be on the ground in shards. I may fear God will forget all about me or I'm beyond repair. I can argue with him, criticize his methods, and question his heart. I can stage a rebellion and attempt to take over the wheel.

I can shut down my heart to him and follow other lovers who promise to give me what I think I want.

The imagery in the question suggests God is accustomed to the clay talking back to him.

Clay: "What in the world are you making? This can't be right! Ach, you're hurting me. Let me off this wheel right now!"

God: "Don't you know I love you and my creations are exquisite? Trust me and you will love the finished product."

In my own way, I have interrogated the potter. I have visited his studio and found him working on *other* pots. I've pointed out a rough edge he's missed or a marred surface that needs attention. He might even give me a turn at the wheel. "Want to help? Just follow my instructions."

When I cannot get his attention, I've tried to "help" anyway. I've even taken over the wheel to fix the one little thing he's missed that bugs me. My interference never seems to work. But later, in spite of my meddling—*voila!*—a perfect and beautiful pot is produced.

The description of the potter's house also suggests that some pots have been so damaged that they are mere fragments. What about those broken pieces?

Here's an example of someone I know. I'll call my friend "Jane." She was a little girl, full of joy, full of adventure, fearless, and happy. But she was sexually abused and then kept that dark secret for thirty years. A seed of shame was planted that grew and grew until it threatened to choke off her very life. She lost access to her true self—the joyful, adventurous little girl she had been. That dazzling child was still there but often covered up with a prickly, yet fragile, exterior.

How does God deal with clay that has been so damaged?

How does he deal with clay that is cynical, angry, or brittle?

God set his heart on delivering Israel from captivity and he moved heaven and earth to accomplish it. He will do no less for those of us who have been enticed away from him or are held captive. He can rescue those whose hearts have been wounded by evil and find themselves in a dark and lonely place. He can come into every dark place and the time of our wounding with his powerful love and grace.

Here's what he promised to do for Cyrus:

> "I will go before you and will level the mountains. I will break down gates of bronze and cut through bars of iron. I will give you the treasures of darkness and riches stored in secret places."
>
> *(Isaiah 45: 2-3)*

He will do no less for my friend. Or for you.

Prayer

Lord,

You are the great creator. You create extraordinary beauty. Even with the divine revelation of your word, it is hard for me to fathom your glory and your glorious plans for creation much less your vision for me. Casting my lot with anything or anyone else would leave me bereft, and would truly, in the end, be only an illusion.

I am in your hands. And I trust you.

Amen

Settle down in the presence of the Lord and meditate on this question, "Does the clay say to the potter, 'What are you making?'" Reflect about whatever comes to mind. Take time later to contemplate the questions in Further Reflections and the Bible verses below.

Does the clay say to the potter, "What are you making?"?

Further Reflections

1. If you believed God intended to mold or remold you in such a way as to create or restore your glory, can you begin to imagine what that might look like?

2. God moved Cyrus' heart. How and when has God moved your heart? You can always ask him to.

Lectio Divina

Romans 12:2 (J.B. Phillips)

Don't let the world around you squeeze you into its own mould, but let God re-mould your mind from within.

Psalm 18: 20-24 (The Message translation)

God made my life complete when I placed all the pieces before him.

When I got my act together, he gave me a fresh start.

Now I'm alert to God's ways; I don't take God for granted.

Everyday I review the way he works; I try not to miss a trick.

I feel put back together, and I'm watching my step.

God rewrote the text of my life when I opened the book of my heart to his eyes.

Chapter 30

Is this not the kind of fasting I have chosen?

"Is this not the kind of fasting I have chosen: to loose the chains of injustice and untie the cords of the yoke, to set the oppressed free and break every yoke?

… to share food with the hungry,

… to provide shelter,

… to clothe the naked,

… not to turn away from your own flesh and blood?"

Isaiah 58:6-7

Fasting is an ancient religious ritual practiced by people of many faiths. People fast for lots of reasons—to cleanse the body and the soul, to set aside time for prayer, and to get control of their appetites. They fast from meat for reasons of conscience, from sugar to improve their health or lose weight, and from alcohol because they know they need to slow down their intake.

Others fast when facing a crossroads in life, or when they're in special need of direction. Catholics and Episcopalians fast to observe the sacred religious season of Lent. Some people fast when seeking a physical healing. A few devout folks regularly fast, setting aside daily bread to seek the hidden bread of God.

If we are desperate, we might not even want to eat, rather we focus all our energy on seeking God, or on fretting, or both. If we are intent on seeking God as we pray for a breakthrough of his kingdom in our circumstances, fasting can help us clarify our situation and reduce the noise and distraction that gets in the way of hearing God.

Fasting can free up a lot of time. It's not just the skipped meal, it's all the preparation and clean-up time, too. Fasting allows time for reflection, time to seek God when we need him more than we need food.

In the situation at hand, the Israelites fasted, prayed, and cried out to God for help. Powerful enemy forces threatened them. They were afraid, so they sought God's intervention on their behalf.

It wasn't working.

"Why have we fasted," they said, "and you have not seen it?

Why have we humbled ourselves and you have not noticed?" (*Isaiah 58:3*)

They might as well have said, "You're not keeping up your end of the bargain."

The ones not keeping up their end of the bargain were really those who fasted and cried out to God for a rescue, the self-serving, dishonest, and depraved leaders, and the ones who followed them with no reluctance whatsoever. The problem was that, although they fasted, they did not address the heart of the matter.

If fasting were just a renouncement of food for a time, most anyone can do that. No change of habits or attitudes is required. If theirs was an attempt to barter with God, it did not work.

Another way to put God's question: "Is this the kind of fasting I want? Religious rituals that leave you just as stubborn and selfish as you were before? You think you have me over a barrel because you've fasted?"

The idea that religious activity could obligate God to intervene on their behalf—a kind of *quid pro quo*—was their temptation. It was an attempt to control God himself.

Today when some people, religious or secular, want to get attention and obtain some kind of political action on their behalf, they might fast. Only they call it a hunger strike. It's their attempt to get the authorities to capitulate. Sometimes it works.

Would a hunger strike work with God? I don't think so.

The heart of the matter was this: they fasted, at least they went through the ritual of fasting, but at the same time they kept quarrelling, exploiting, and physically abusing others (*Isaiah 58:3*). "You cannot fast as you do today and expect to be heard on high" (*Isaiah 58:4*).

God spelled out the kind of fasting he wanted: Stop exploiting! Feed the hungry, clothe the naked, provide shelter for the poor! He wanted concrete actions prompted from a compassionate heart. God wanted a holy lifestyle, not an empty ritual.

God goes on to tell his people through his prophet that if they fast his way, if they change their *hearts*, "Then your light will break forth like the dawn, and your healing will quickly appear… Then you will call and the Lord will answer; you will cry for help and he will say: "Here am I" (*Isaiah 58:8-9*).

To sacrifice something you love in order to to earn God's favor is a mythic pattern. Many early religions made sacrificial offerings to insure a good harvest or fertile livestock. The practice persists in some cultures, and our own offers even more sophisticated versions.

I've done something like this: I gave up something I treasured. God did not tell me to do it; I just thought I "should." Only later did I realize I had an unconscious expectation that God would be proud of me for being so unattached to a material object, and maybe I expected to earn his favor in return.

Even when we know in our heads that God loves us, sometimes we suspect there is some act, creed, ritual, or gift by which we can earn his favors—and maybe get what we want. The key to "right" fasting is not our outward actions but our inner motives and our hearts.

Nothing in this passage or the question suggests God is against fasting. What he's against is hypocrisy.

Nothing suggests fasting is ineffective. God does help, rescue, save, deliver, heal, and intervene. He does it over and over again, but if we sacrifice something in order to force God's hand, with no accompanying change of heart, it won't work.

Fasting is an act of self-denial. It can be done in the service of getting attention or in the service of paying attention. Maybe at least one point of fasting is to elicit compassion for those who don't have the means to obtain what we are giving up.

Prayer

Father,

I humbly implore you to show me what habits or indulgences I allow myself that are thwarting my life and are not pleasing to you. What am I doing or failing to do that impedes your Spirit from full access to all of me?

Please save me from empty rituals and any kind of hypocrisy. I want to be transparent—no hidden sins from you or from me.

Please give me a heart of compassion for those who are hungry.

Amen

Settle down in the presence of the Lord and meditate on this question, "Is this not the kind of fasting I have chosen?" Reflect about whatever comes to mind. Take time later to contemplate the questions in Further Reflections and the Bible verses below.

Is this not the kind of fasting I have chosen?

Further Reflections

1. Are you called to a fast? A permanent fast? What's the one thing you don't want to give up, even for awhile? Try fasting from that for a day. You might see how attached to it you are.

2. Instead of giving something up for awhile, is there some spiritual practice you might want to try for a season, for instance, contemplation, lectio divina, or praying with a friend? Or perhaps something more outward, serving at a soup kitchen, tutoring underprivileged kids, giving to the man on the street you pass everyday on your way to work, etc. Which of these options most appeals to you? Try doing it everyday for a week or two.

Lectio Divina

Matthew 6:16-18
   "When you fast, do not look somber as the hypocrites do, for they disfigure their faces to show men they are fasting. I tell you the truth; they have received their reward in full. But when you fast, put oil on your head and wash your face, so that it will not be obvious to men that you are fasting, but only to your Father, who is unseen; and your Father who sees what is done in secret, will reward you."

I Samuel 16:7

The Lord does not look at the things people look at. People look at the outward appearance, but the Lord looks at the heart.

Chapter 31

Has this house that bears my name become a den of thieves to you?

Will you steal and murder, commit adultery and perjury, burn incense to Baal and follow other gods you have not known and then come and stand before me in this house which bears my Name and say, "We are safe"—safe to do all these detestable things? Has this house that bears my Name become a den of thieves to you?

Jeremiah 7:9-11

The circumstances here are similar to the previous scenario when God confronted the people about their fasting practices. They committed terrible offenses, but still expected a rescue. Now, instead of religious rituals, they think the temple will keep them safe. They believed they would be safe in Jerusalem because Solomon's temple was there. The idea was that God would never allow his temple to be destroyed, so if they stayed near it, they would be safe. False prophets fed this false sense of security.

In spite of violating God's laws, (oppressing foreigners, orphans and widows, committing murder, adultery, perjury, and chasing after false gods), they thought if they ran to the temple when their enemies attacked, they would be safe, as though the temple offered magical protection.

The question God posed suggested the response. The temple that bears the Name and holds the Presence had become a den of thieves. Superficial fasting produced no spiritual results. Clinging to the temple (or any religious institution), while their hearts remained far from the Lord, and continuing their abominable practices, would afford no real protection.

Instead, God *allowed* their sins to catch up to them. He exposed them to the consequences to wake them up. If their faith was in the temple (or a church, denomination, pastor, or priest) instead of the Lord, who was to be worshipped in the temple, then he just might assent to destruction of the temple: a rather dramatic wake-up call. Not too much later, the temple was destroyed.

When he turned the courtyard in the temple upside-down and drove out the thieves of his day, Jesus quoted this passage about the den of thieves. They had established a profane market on sacred ground. Nobody else seemed concerned about the money changers' profits from selling the sacrificial animals. It was business (or corruption) as usual and raised nary an eyebrow. What Jesus did to these "thieves" soon made the authorities so angry they were ready to kill him; he was, after all, interfering with their economy.

Then as today, two kinds of thieves can be in the temple: external and internal. External thieves are often obvious. They create the headlines. We all hear of the scandals that erupt when church leaders are discovered abusing their sheep, exploiting their position, or stealing from the offering. The stories of the sexual abuse of children, the theft of their innocence, sickens us. The authorities compound the sin by covering it up.

How could they! Do they think they are protecting the church, or maybe the church, the institution, should, as if by magic, protect them? Less dramatic are the televangelists who promise the favor of God in exchange for "an offering of any amount." According to Jeremiah, this misappropriation is nothing new and still gives a black eye to the whole church.

Internal thieves hide out on the inside of us. In the Old Testament, the temple housed the Presence of God. Jesus expanded that, teaching that we ourselves, our bodies, can host the Presence. We can each become a temple.

So this question can be put to us as individuals. What thieves have we allowed to set up shop in our lives? Any sin can become a slave-driver. Lies we believe can rob us of peace and faith. Fear can be a thief when it robs us of faith in God and peace of mind. Hypocrisy is definitely a thief. It interferes with an honest an open relationship with God and others, too. Addictions are always thieves. Even innocent-looking preoccupations can steal our potential intimacy with God and our loved ones. Jesus described the enemy of our souls as "*the* thief" (*John 10:10*, ital. added).

What practices and behaviors happen under our noses, or worse yet, are ones we participate in, that are offensive to God? We need to see what holy ground we have not kept holy. Can we realign with Jesus by overturning the thieves lurking in or around us?

Ezekiel wrote an interesting account of something that happened around the same time. An angel of the Lord showed Ezekiel a vision of the glory of God in the temple. Angels and smoke filled the temple until it was radiant. The Lord arose from his throne and moved to the threshold; the angels followed. After a pause, the angels, the glory, and the Lord himself withdrew from the temple. They moved outside the city and stopped above the mountain east of it (*Ezekiel 10:4-11:23*). The divine glory departed the temple and, except for Ezekiel, nobody even noticed.

The glory left in stages—almost with reluctance—due to too much corruption and apostasy. Religious activity continued as usual, the priests and the people did not abandon their rituals, but God was not present. The people were either so preoccupied they didn't notice or so corrupt they didn't care. In either case, they couldn't tell the difference between God's presence in the temple or his absence.

God promises to be a refuge for those who seek him. Jesus promises never to leave us or forsake us. We can, however, still leave him or at least live our lives without any thought of him. We can go about our lives and even our religious activities and at the same time ignore God. We can leave him out of our worship even if we call ourselves believers.

What thieves, what money changers, have set up shop (or attempted to) in your soul and crowded out the Presence of God? They might not look like thieves at all.

Prayer

Father,

Your word tells me that my heart is your dwelling place, that your spirit sanctifies me and makes me a temple of your Presence. I believe it and I welcome you.

Your word also tells me that I have an enemy, a thief who would kill, steal, and destroy my life. So I know a den of thieves is really a stronghold of "the thief."

God, please turn over the tables in my heart and drive out every last thief. I love your Presence.

Amen

Settle down in the presence of the Lord and meditate on this question, "Has this house that bears my name become a den of thieves to you?" Reflect about whatever comes to mind. Take time later to contemplate the questions in Further Reflections and the Bible verses below.

Has this house that bears my name become a den of thieves to you?

Further Reflections

1. Where, how and when have you experienced the presence of God? Do you carry a sense of his presence within you?

2. What can you undertake to make a more spacious place for the spirit of God within you?

Lectio Divina

Mark 11:15-18

On reaching Jerusalem, Jesus entered the temple and began driving out those who were buying and selling there. He overturned the tables of the money changers and the benches of those selling doves, and would not allow anyone to carry merchandise through the temple courts. And as he taught them, he said, "Is it not written: 'My house will be called a house of prayer for all the nations?' But you have made it a den of robbers." The chief priests and the teachers of the law heard this and began looking for a way to kill him, for they feared him, because the whole crowd was amazed at this teaching.

I Corinthians 6:19

Do you not know that your bodies are temples of the Holy Spirit, who is in you, whom you have received from God? You are not your own.

Chapter 32

Are they not harming themselves to their own shame?

"Do you not see what they are doing in the towns of Judah and on the streets of Jerusalem? The children gather wood, the fathers light the fire, and the women knead the dough and make cakes of bread for the Queen of Heaven, [Ishtar]. They pour out drink offerings to other gods to provoke me to anger. But am I the one they are provoking?" declares the Lord. "Are they not rather harming themselves, to their own shame?"

Jeremiah 7:17-19

God's people became infatuated with Ishtar, one of the Babylonian gods. They blatantly broke the first commandment: "I am the Lord your God, who brought you out of Egypt, out of the land of slavery. You shall have no other gods before me." (*Exodus 20:2-3*).

God saw it all: fathers, mothers, and even children, gathering wood, lighting fires, and offering bread and drink to the foreign god. God asked whether they had so misjudged him and his character that they thought his jealousy of other gods was all about him. "Are they not rather harming themselves?" Their actions did not "harm" God.

To recap: just a few weeks after Moses led them in their escape from slavery, God made a covenant with his people. He gave Moses the Ten Commandments—the blueprint for their new society. They would obey him and he would be their God always. The purpose of the law: "Walk in the way that the Lord your God has commanded you, *so that you may live and prosper and prolong your days in the land you will possess*" (*Deuteronomy 5:33*, ital. added).

The point of the law was not to make his people excel at rule keeping; rather it was to insure an exceptional and prosperous life. God not only gave them ten commandments to live by, he also told them, over and over, "Choose life" (*Deuteronomy 30:19*).

Life was the goal, not rule-keeping. Under the Mosaic covenant, the Lord would be the Israelites' God, they would be his people, and the outward manifestation of this new relationship—the law and their obedience to it—would result in a blessed life.

Pagan cultures, ones that worshipped a number of different gods, surrounded Israel, and the Israelites wanted to join in their rituals and religious observances. What was the harm? Worshipping Baal involved orgies and sex with temple prostitutes. Worshipping Molech included sacrificing children in fire to insure prosperity.

These were not good gods! Modern "gods" don't require child sacrifice, but that does not mean that our idols don't require some kind of oblation. Idols today can still be demanding taskmasters. God links the first commandment, not to have any other gods, with their deliverance from slavery. Serving other gods would lead them (and us) right back into servitude.

Once we have another god, it reorders our whole life. We become like the one we spend time with, the one we worship. We can become great and good or shallow and materialistic, loving and truthful or angry and deceitful, full of the spirit of grace and peace or full of fear and cravings. We can trust in the true unseen God or we can trust in a guru, even a celebrity, or our own magic formulas and rituals.

Today we don't bow down to Baal, but we might ask what we bow down to in his place. What do we worship with our time, money, thoughts, and dreams? How does what we worship harm us?

In *The Lord of the Rings*, Golem worshipped the magic ring; he called it "my precious." He became obsessed with it and its power. Bit by bit, it destroyed him.

That is the way obsession works. That is why it matters whom you love and whom and what you worship. Another example is seen in *The Wolf of Wall Street*, the movie based on the life of Jordan Belfort, who made millions at others' expense, money he used on drugs to the ruin of his family. Money was his god. His life was a lightning-fast rise and fall. The film portrays the excesses of modern life. Granted, it's over the top; much of our idol worship is more discreet than Jordan Belfort's. In fact, we don't always recognize it and, when we do, we likely don't think it is harmful to us or anyone else. We believe we have it under control.

Religious cults provide a clear picture of how someone can harm himself by worshipping other gods. Whatever else they are or say they are, they are dictatorships. It's not that the Branch Davidians, the Scientologists, or the followers of Jim Jones don't or didn't have some worthy goals about love, honesty, or accepting yourself or others, it's that the price of membership seems to be loss of personal freedom and the right to disagree with the leader.

Paul says you become the slave of the one you choose to obey (*Romans 6:16*). But that is not true—it does not happen—when we love God with all our heart and obey him. God does not have slavery in mind for those who are obedient to him. Instead of a spirit of slavery, he sends the spirit of his son into the hearts of those who believe in him. "So you are no longer a slave but a son; and since you are a son, God has also made you an heir" (*Galatians 4:7*).

Some may find offensive the idea of God being jealous of other gods, as though he is a petty tyrant. If God just wants us to bow and scrape, that might be true. But God is in covenant with us, and if we betray him for someone or something else, then that disloyalty is a break in the relationship, just like it is when we betray a spouse or a best friend. God's question suggests that the betrayal harms us in ways we cannot fathom. God's goal is our flourishing and our holiness. His goal is our freedom. Obedience is involved, but not blind, lock-step compliance. It's just like in the best of human relationships—we do things for those we love from a heart of love.

We are his children and he has gifts to give us. We are "heirs." He takes this very seriously. Our hearts are at stake. The commandments are not given to kill our joy, but to save our lives. Most of us don't join cults, many of us are not religious at all, but lots of us worship something, value it, and sacrifice for it. What we worship can set us on a trajectory of ultimate freedom and joy… or the opposite.

Prayer

Father,

There is no way I can be vigilant enough to guard against idols because I don't always recognize them as fake or as "gods," much less see the harm. You tell me I'm playing with fire and I believe you.

So please tell me about the gods I serve without even knowing I'm doing it, and tell me about the ones my whole culture has adopted, because they can look deceptively innocent.

You truly are the one, true God.

Amen

Settle down in the presence of the Lord and meditate on this question, "Are you not harming yourself to your own shame?" Reflect about whatever comes to mind. Take time later to contemplate the questions in Further Reflections and the Bible verses below.

Are you harming yourself to your own shame?

Further Reflections

1. What do you long for most in life? Does it seem a worthy goal for your heart? In your heart of hearts, where does God stand in relation to the objects you desire?

2. Is there a connection between something you have idolized and a sense of shame?

Lectio Divina

Deuteronomy 29:18
  Make sure there is no man or woman, clan or tribe among you today whose heart turns away from the Lord your God to go and worship the gods of those nations; make sure there is no root among you that produces such bitter poison.

Psalm 115: 4-8
  But their idols are silver and gold,
  made by the hands of men.
  They have mouths but cannot speak,
  eyes, but they cannot see;
  They have hands, but cannot feel,
  feet but they cannot walk.;
  nor can they utter a sound with their throats.
  Those who make them will be like them,
  and so will all who trust in them.

Chapter 33

Do I not fill heaven and earth?

"Am I only a God nearby," declared the Lord, "and not a God far away? Can anyone hide in secret places so that I cannot see him?" declares the Lord. "Do not I fill heaven and earth?" declares the Lord.

Jeremiah 23:23-24

In times past, it had been important to God to teach his people that he was close by, that he was with them individually and personally. They needed to learn he was not like the gods worshipped long ago, gods who were thought to be confined to a geographic location.

For example, the moon god might only have dominion in Ur, the god of the Nile in Egypt, and so on. It was a revelation to Jacob when he was on the run from Esau that the Lord promised to be with him—even as he ran away from Canaan to Haran. "I am with you and will watch over you wherever you go, and I will bring you back to this land. I will not leave you until I have done what I have promised you" (*Genesis 28:15*).

Not only would he be *with* Jacob, he would protect him *wherever* he went. He promised Moses he would be with him when he sent him back to Egypt. God would/could be present in any geographic location.

By the time of Jeremiah, God had established his dwelling on earth in the temple in Jerusalem. The people thought of God as living in the temple and, before that, in the Ark of the Covenant. It was comforting to know God encamped with them. He had a "home" on earth.

Some of the Israelites, however, came to think that if they dabbled in evil *away* from the temple, then God wouldn't notice. God made it clear that whatever your theological understanding about where God is, there really is no hiding place. God is everywhere and over all; he is able to see all. Our faith or lack of faith does not dictate his sovereignty or his presence. The temple may hold his Presence, but the whole world is equally his domain.

Why was this important? Many people were in full rebellion against God. Through the prophet Jeremiah, he was attempting to guide those who were on the wrong track back to him. However, there were other "prophets" also claiming to hear from God. They told the people what they wanted to hear, to wit, that they could keep behaving however they wanted; they could worship others gods without consequences.

God was angry at these "false" prophets and this question was also directed to them. Did they really think he didn't see what they were up to, or he didn't hear their deceptive promises? He told Jeremiah he had neither spoken to them, nor sent them. They were making up their visions, dreams, and messages— they were not from the Lord. He did not condone any of this (*Jeremiah 23*).

I have a contemporary example. I know someone, a priest, who believed that once a year it was okay to indulge in just about anything you wanted to do. You could do forbidden things as though God would oblige you by looking the other way. He described it as a kind of Mardi Gras or king's x for otherwise religious people. His attitude seemed to be, if it was just once a year, what could be the harm? He wanted to believe God wouldn't notice or even care, if it was so infrequent. He was sure he would get a free pass. Self-indulgent, yes, but he also invited others to participate in soul-damaging practices, and he found listeners who loved this message.

It's less clear why the false prophets in Jeremiah's account would make up "prophecies" to mislead others. Maybe they were merely misguided, but they might have been self-indulgent, too.

Some people go to great lengths to search out a prophet (or pastor or priest or guru) who will tell them what they want to hear. The problem is that when someone tells us what we want to hear, and we keep listening, *and they're wrong,* we will get lost and not know it. We can even get very smug about our "enlightenment," but we will be on the wrong track. Jesus called this "the blind leading the blind" (*Matthew 15:14*).

Some people like the idea of a remote God. Their answer to God's question is, "Yes, you are far away and please stay there." The flip side to the convenience of a distant God is this: what do you do when you need him most? What do you do when your way has produced heartache and you need a god who *does* see you?

When I was a girl, I read a wonderful little book by Robert Munger, *My Heart, Christ's Home.* It imagined someone inviting Christ into her life and he came in "room by room." The front rooms—the living room and dining room—were already in order. The other rooms, however, needed to be cleaned out. One room in the back of the house was locked and off-limits. It took a while before Christ was invited into this dark and dirty space. When he was allowed in, his light dispelled the darkness and he set the room in order. The premise of the book was that Christ will wait to be asked before entering our locked rooms, (even when he knows they are secreting things that are harmful to our souls, memories of trauma, pain and shame), but he will come where invited and set things right.

God will dress our wounds, speak bracing truth, heal our souls, and "sup with us." If we think God doesn't see our hidden rooms, we are fooling ourselves, and we have no idea how much our secrets cost us. These are the spaces that most need the fresh light and wind of his spirit. Think of the dark rooms as filled with a cancer that grows in secret and destroys at a slow pace. We rejoice in surgical cures. That is what God offers to our souls.

Whether we like it or not, we cannot hide from God. There really is no secret place. This can produce relief or resentment. Can you imagine the relief of at last surrendering the keys to everything to him? As John Eldridge states, there is an utter relief to holiness.

Prayer

Father,

You know everything, and nothing is hidden from your sight. Your spirit hovers over the chaos in my life the same way it did in the beginning. You spoke: "Let there be light." Let your light touch my whole life: every memory, every thought, circumstance and relationship and every dark place.

Illumine me. In your light I see light, even where there once was darkness. Thank you for the grace of seeing me.

Amen

Settle down in the presence of the Lord and meditate on this question, "Do I not fill heaven and earth?" Reflect about whatever comes to mind. Take time later to contemplate the questions in Further Reflections and the Bible verses below.

Do I not fill heaven and earth?

Further Reflections

1. When you think of God, do you see him at a great distance or close by? How do you feel about your secrets not being secret from him?

2. Knowing he already knows, can you tell him the secrets of your life?

Lectio Divina

Psalm 139:8-12
>Where can I go from your Spirit?
>Where can I flee from your presence?
>If I go up to the heavens, you are there;
>if I make my bed in the depths, you are there.
>If I rise on the wings of the dawn,
>if I settle on the far side of the sea,
>even there your hand will guide me;
>your right hand will hold me fast.
>If I say, "Surely the darkness will hide me and the light becomes night around me,"
>even the darkness will not be dark to you;
>the night will shine like the day,
>for darkness is as light to you.

Acts 17:24-25

The God who made the world and everything in it is the Lord of heaven and earth and does not live in temples built by human hands. And he is not served by human hands, as if he needed anything, because he himself gives all men life and breath and everything else.

Chapter 34

Is anything too hard for me?

See how the siege ramps are built up to take the city. Because of the sword, famine and plague, the city will be handed over to the Babylonians who are attacking it. What you said has happened, as you now see. And though the city will be handed over to the Babylonians, you, O Sovereign Lord, say to me, "Buy the field with silver and have the transaction witnessed."

Then the word of the Lord came to Jeremiah: "I am the Lord, the God of all Mankind. Is anything too hard for me?"

Jeremiah 32:24-27

God told Jeremiah the Babylonians were coming and they would attack, pillage, take captives, and destroy Jerusalem. Jeremiah warned the king and leaders of this threat, but instead of being grateful for the warning, the king was furious. It was not what he wanted to hear. The king still listened to the false prophets who were proclaiming that none of these dire predictions would come to pass.

In the middle of this standoff between Jeremiah and the king, with the enemy getting closer and closer, the Lord gave Jeremiah an instruction. He told him his cousin would come to him with an offer to sell him his field. The next day that is what happened. Jeremiah realized God intended him to buy the field, so he signed the deed and paid the money.

But in truth, what was the point of buying property when the whole country was on the brink of war and Jeremiah had already been told that Judah would lose? What Jeremiah really wanted to know was: why buy the field?

God said, "Is anything too hard for me?"

The Lord then told Jeremiah what he had in mind. Yes, the Babylonians will ransack the country, they will take many captives and destroy the temple, but this real estate transaction will survive long after Judah's defeat. One day Jeremiah's heirs will inherit this land. One day God will gather his scattered children, he will bring them out of captivity and return them to their home. The old covenant may be over, but God will make a new covenant with his people, an everlasting covenant. He will never stop doing good to them. His people will once again live in safety in their own land.

The field Jeremiah bought was a token; it was a stake in the future. It was an investment and a promise: no matter how bleak the circumstances, this was not the end because nothing is too hard for the Lord.

Jeremiah was not the first to hear this question, "Is anything too hard for me?" God asked Moses if his arm was so short that it could not save, implying that no problem is beyond his strength or his reach. He asked Abraham and Sarah why they laughed when he promised them a child in their old age and assured them nothing was too hard (or too wonderful) for him.

The patriarchs needed encouragement, and now Jeremiah needed encouragement, too. God's question dared him to believe in a future he could not fathom.

And yet, what God told Jeremiah to do was audacious. Judah was about to be defeated by a very powerful nation, and God wanted him to buy a field? He might need that silver for something else much more important (and more rational).

But the real estate transaction was a sign to Jeremiah and to the people who witnessed it. Houses, fields, and vineyards would once again be bought and sold. A happy ending would follow the sad chapter of defeat and captivity. Buying the land was an enacted parable meant to give hope to all the people.

This is what the Lord says:

> "As I have brought all this calamity on this people, so I will give them all the prosperity I have promised them. Once more fields will be bought in this land of which you say, 'It is a desolate waste, without men or animals, for it has been handed over to the Babylonians.' Fields will be bought for silver, and deeds will be signed,

sealed, and witnessed in the territory of Benjamin,
in the villages around Jerusalem and in the towns of
the hill country, of the western foothills and of the
Negev, because I will restore their fortunes, declares the
Lord."

Jeremiah 32:42-44

God's way of dealing with this hopeless situation was to have Jeremiah spend his dwindling resources on a land deal. In a similar story, he instructed Elijah to tell a widow to take her meager resources to make him a cake. She miraculously ended up having the means to live for years to come. Jesus took a boy's lunch and fed thousands of hungry people.

In all these instances, the Lord called for an eccentric test of faith, not a test of believing the right doctrine but of believing and trusting him. When the world falls apart, God reminds us, sometimes in outlandish ways, that nothing is too hard for him. The worst was about to happen to Judah, but redemption waited just around the corner.

God set this pattern for his people, so maybe we can trust that when disaster strikes, a good end will still be in store for us, too.

Prayer

Father,

I love this story. Thank you that you recognize how much I need hope, too. When I was discouraged, this passage became a personal message to me. I love to see your hand in my circumstances.

Thank you that you don't begrudge us signs of hope. Keep me awake and aware. I don't want to miss a thing.

Amen

Settle down in the presence of the Lord and meditate on this question, "Is anything too hard for the Lord?" Reflect about whatever comes to mind. Take time later to contemplate the questions in Further Reflections and the Bible verses below.

Is anything too hard for the Lord?

Further Reflections

1. Have you been given a sign of hope in the middle of terrible circumstances?

2. When you were a child, how did the adults in your life handle difficult circumstances?

Lectio Divina

Jeremiah 33:10-11
This is what the Lord says, "You say about this place, 'It is a desolate waste without men or animals.' Yet in the towns of Judah and the streets of Jerusalem that are deserted, inhabited by neither men nor animals, there will be heard once more the sounds of joy and gladness, the voices of bride and bridegroom, and the voices of those who bring thank offerings to the house of the Lord saying, 'Give thanks to the Lord Almighty, for the Lord is good; his love endures forever.' For I will restore the fortunes of the land as they were before," says the Lord.

Ephesians 3:20-21
Now to him who is able to do immeasurably more than all we ask or imagine, according to his power that is at work within us, to him be the glory in the church and in Christ Jesus throughout all generations, forever and ever! Amen

PART 6

THE PROPHETS IN RELATION TO GOD

Chapters 35 - 40

As God speaks to his prophets, each question reveals more of God's character and personality. We learn what he focuses on and cares about. Some of the questions in this section are posed to or about the people of Israel. Some arise out of God's personal relationship with the prophets themselves. After all, they are his children, too. Indeed, they are on intimate terms with him. They are loyal to God, and he draws close to them. He wants them to see what he is doing and to participate in the new kingdom he plans. They have a part to play.

Only a handful of prophets lived at any given time in the Old Testament, but God promised to pour out his spirit on all people one day. Many will prophecy, dream dreams, and see visions (*Joel 2:28*).

The prophets in the old testament were forerunners of the

kind of relationship we can all have with God. Sometimes he speaks to us, and other times he might give us a message for someone else.

Before you look at the questions in this section, meditate for a few minutes on having a holy or consecrated imagination, as well as hidden meanings, dreams, and visions.

Reflect on significant recurring dreams you may have had. Consider all the ways God might communicate with you.

Chapter 35

Do I take pleasure in the death of the wicked?

"But if a wicked man turns away from all the sins he has committed and keeps all my decrees and does what is just and right, he will surely live; he will not die. None of the offenses he has committed will be remembered against him. Because of the righteous things he has done, he will live. Do I take any pleasure in the death of the wicked? declares the sovereign Lord. Rather, am I not pleased when they turn from their ways and live?"

Ezekiel 18:21-23

God discussed with Ezekiel the consequences of sin and tried to make clear to him that when one turns away from unrighteousness, God remembers his sins no more. The question itself, "Does God take pleasure in the death of the wicked?" was very important at that time because all Israel bore the consequence of its unrighteousness: Babylon had, at last, conquered it. Many had died and many others had been taken back to Babylon, including Ezekiel.

In an attempt both to warn and elicit a change of heart, prophets had earlier predicted their defeat and exile. The warnings hadn't worked. Their stubborness and unfaithfulnes resulted in their current capitivity.

Now they were bereft and wondered how God felt about them. Did God delight in their downfall? Was God *happy* they had been taken captive? They were homesick, in fact, they grieved for home. "By the rivers of Babylon we sat and wept when we remembered Zion" (*Psalm 137:1*). They wondered if God had turned against them forever—was he so angry that he would have nothing more to do with them? Was there still a chance of redemption and return? So to the men, women, and children living in exile, the question, "What is God's heart toward me now?" was very important.

The question goes to the heart of faith, of who God is, and who we believe him to be. Does he ever take pleasure in the death or suffering of even the most wicked? Does he take pleasure in their punishment?

Any good parent must discipline her children from time

to time. We know discipline does not negate love, and our children seem to know this as well. Children want and need a strong parent to set things right. However, if a child suspected that his mom or dad relished meting out consequences for bad behavior, that would alter the whole relationship.

If we believe it pleases God to bring punishment to the wicked, then we can become vigilantes on God's behalf, performing "religious" duties on those we deem to be wicked. If we find ourselves in the hot seat, if we have become one of the wicked, and we believe God delights in our downfall, then how or why would we ever want to turn back to him?

The problem is that sometimes we project onto God our own thoughts and feelings. We take pleasure when someone gets what he deserves. We love a good scandal and a deserved comeuppance. If God is like us, we are in trouble. Yet he answers his own question so there will be no doubt in our hearts—no suspicion of his will toward us. "For I take no pleasure in the death of anyone declares the Sovereign Lord. Repent and live" (*Ezekiel 18:32*).

God is happy when we repent, when we turn away from evil and side with him, because when we choose him, we choose life. The extravagant gift and abundance of life, the tree of life, is God's will for us. Jesus said, "But I have come to give you everything in abundance, more than you expect—life in its fullness until you overflow!" (*John 10:10*, The Passion Translation). Sometimes the consequences we face can be the most direct road back to that life.

We are his children, so maybe the most helpful way to think about God involves remembering he is a parent. Think about the grief of parents when a wayward son or daughter breaks the law and is thrown in jail. Even if they hope this teaches a lesson, they are so sad at what's become of them. Imagine the joy when that child comes to himself and returns home as the one we once knew. Consider the anguish parents feel when they have to say no to a child who has abused their trust. It goes against the grain. However, saying "no" can lead to an awakening much more powerful than all our "help."

The people of God had sinned and rebelled against him for years and now suffered severe consequences. They had lost their homeland, exiled like Adam and Eve before them and like their forefathers who were slaves in Egypt. They were miserable. They had no power against their oppressors. They knew they had sinned, but the only comfort that would help could only come from the one they had sinned against.

Their only hope was the word of God, written and also spoken through Ezekiel and the other prophets of the era. God made promises to them! He still had plans for them! He was not happy about their predicament. He promised to rescue them and bring them home.

Have you or someone close to you experienced a radical transformation? Sometimes that comes after we hit rock bottom. Sometimes we have to lose it all—the job, the marriage, the reputation—to find the hidden treasure of God's love. If you have experienced God's love in person, it becomes easier to believe that he takes no pleasure in the death of the wicked. It becomes easier to believe you are indeed beloved, everyone else is as well, and his banner over us is love. To believe God is love.

Even when punishment is a consequence of what we have done, God has made it clear he is for us. If we have been taken captive by our enemy through our own pride or folly, his heart is still with us. These are two of the promises made by God to the Israelites in captivity:

> This is what the sovereign Lord says: "When seventy years are completed in Babylon, I will come to you and fulfill my gracious promise to bring you back to this place. For I know the plans I have for you," declares the Lord, "plans to prosper you and not to harm you, plans to give you hope and a future."
>
> *Jeremiah 29:10*

He will search for us and bring us to him.

> For this is what the sovereign says: "I myself will search for my sheep and look after them. As a shepherd looks after his scattered flock when he is with them, so will I look after my sheep. I will rescue them from all the places where they were scattered on a day of clouds and darkness."
>
> *Ezekiel 34: 11-12*

Prayer

Father,

I'm so glad you are who you are. Thank you so much for your steadfast love for me.

Please make my heart to be like yours. I want to drink deeply of your living water, to rejoice with others when they are happy and weep with them when they are heartbroken, to dance at weddings and cry at funerals. Please tell me what pleases you about me and likewise what annoys you about me. I trust your unfailing love.

Thank you for the great gift of life.

Amen

Settle down in the presence of the Lord and meditate on this question, "Do I take pleasure in the death of the wicked?" Reflect about whatever comes to mind. Take time later to contemplate the questions in Further Reflections and the Bible verses below.

Do I take pleasure in the death of the wicked?

Further Reflections

1. What "discipline" have you experienced as an adult and what have you learned from it?

2. What or who has taken your soul captive? How did that happen and how long did that last? How were you rescued? Do you need a rescue?

Lectio Divina

II Peter 3:9

The Lord is not slow in keeping his promise, as some understand slowness. He is patient with you, not wanting anyone to perish, but everyone to come to repentance.

Psalm 103:8-11 (The Passion Translation)

Lord, you're so kind and tenderhearted to those who don't deserve it

and so patient with people who fail you!

Your love is like a flooding river overflowing its banks with kindness.

You don't look at us only to find faults, just so you can hold a grudge against us.

You may discipline us for our many sins, but never as much as we really deserve.

Nor do you get even with us for what we've done.

Higher than the highest heavens—that's how high your tender mercy extends!

Greater than the grandeur of heaven above is the greatness of your loyal love,

towering over all who fear you and bow down before you!

Chapter 36

Can these bones live?

The hand of the Lord was upon me, and he brought me out by the Spirit of the Lord and set me in the middle of the valley; it was full of bones. He led me back and forth among them, and I saw a great many bones on the floor of the valley, bones that were very dry. He asked me, "Son of man, can these bones live?"

Ezekiel 37:1-3

God continued his message of hope to his people in Babylon. God brought Ezekiel "by the Spirit" and placed him in a valley of dry bones—lots of bones and very dry. No one could miss the implication. By the spirit, Ezekiel saw a vision of Israel, desolate, captive, hopeless, and dried up. Then God said to Ezekiel, "Can these bones live?" Surely that is the question we most need answered when we are holding on by a mere shred of hope, when we feel dead inside or very dry, or when our bleak circumstances overwhelm us.

Ezekiel said with great diplomacy, "O sovereign Lord, you alone know." Certainly in the natural state, it was way too late. They were just bones. Could there be a resuscitation? Then the most amazing thing happened. God invited Ezekiel into the vision. He wanted to use Ezekiel's voice. Here's how he instructed Ezekiel to speak to the bones:

> This is what the Sovereign Lord says to these bones: "I will make breath enter you, and you will come to life. I will attach tendons to you and make flesh come upon you and cover you with skin; I will put breath in you, and you will come to life."
>
> (*Ezekiel 37:5-6*)

Following God's instruction, Ezekiel commanded the bones to be joined together, be covered with skin, and come to life. Sure enough, as Ezekiel spoke, the bones came back together— just like in the children's song, *Them Bones*. But there was no breath in them. God told Ezekiel to call forth the breath (another word for *spirit*), so these slain people, now more or less put back together, could live again.

Again Ezekiel "prophesied," this time to the breath, and the breath complied. "They came to life and stood up on their feet, a vast army" (*Ezekiel 37:10*). It happened first in Ezekiel's vision, then it was a message of hope to those who had lost everything, and as time passed it came true. The Israelites taken captive to Babylon were liberated and given new life.

This movement from bondage to freedom, from death to life, is a template. We've seen the pattern before, and it's a harbinger of the death and resurrection of Jesus that is to come, and, with it, the promise of new life made available to all who would receive him.

This was a vision tailor-made for the Israelites in Babylon, but it is good to know that God is willing to breathe fresh air into our own lives.

Here's a true story about dead bones. One of my best friends married her wonderful college boyfriend. They had a sweet life and a sweet baby. They moved back home where he joined the family business, and she got pregnant with their second baby. It turned out that the family business was not at all what he wanted; he assumed his marriage was to blame for his ensuing depression, and he wanted out. In his twenties, he was having a mid-life crisis.

She asked him to stay until she had the baby and he agreed. But his dark mood persisted, so my friend let him go. They got a divorce just after their little girl was born. The marriage was dead. Her heart was broken.

All of her friends rallied around, and to make her feel better they criticized him and ostracized him, too. Wouldn't you expect her to be a little bitter?

Here's the amazing thing. She wasn't bitter and she wasn't angry. She refused to blame, and she never played the victim. The marriage and her sweet former life were over, but she held onto her faith. She trusted God for her future.

Before long, her ex-husband came to his senses (you could say he came back from the dead). He realized he'd made the biggest mistake of his life and a few months later they remarried. That was over forty years ago, and they are happily married still.

This might be a rare outcome of a divorce, but it's not rare to be given a bitter pill, to lose something you treasure, and yet to find new life on the other side. It's not rare to be betrayed, to lose a job you love, to lose a career, to lose a home, or even a homeland, only to discover the wind of the Spirit blowing away the rubble, blowing life into something dead, and to find fresh life taking root deep inside of you.

This story about Ezekiel was not the first occasion where the Spirit had been breathed into man. Go back to the very genesis of man. God made Adam out of the dust of the earth, then God himself breathed into this clay "and the man became a living being" (*Genesis 2:7*).

Nor will this story in Ezekiel be the last time the Spirit is breathed into mankind. Centuries later, the resurrected Jesus came to his disciples huddled in fear behind locked doors after his crucifixion, their own world blown apart. First he spoke peace to them, then he commissioned them, and then "he breathed on them and said "Receive the Holy Spirit" (*John 20:22*).

The breath of God, the Spirit, always gives life, to man in the beginning, to desiccated bones in Ezekiel's vision, to women and men walking the planet to this day. The Nicene Creed calls this Spirit "the author and giver of life." What an amazing honor for Ezekiel to participate in imparting this fresh life to a people who had lost everything.

In the same way, God calls us to participate in his holy work. Sometimes it is our turn to receive the fresh wind of God. Sometimes it is our turn to call it forth, to speak it over someone who is dead inside.

You may be looking at dead bones in your own life right now and God might be asking you if they can live. Or perhaps you are functioning well enough in your life, but there's no Spirit, no breath of God in you. This story illustrates that God is not just interested in resuscitation or mere functioning. He's interested in life abundant.

Prayer

Lord,

You are the God of hope. I've hit a dead end before, but you did not leave me there. I'm praying for someone who's hit a dead end, too, and I'm confident you hold them in the palm of your hand.

Thank you for the message that you don't forget about dead bones.

Amen

Settle down in the presence of the Lord and meditate on this question,"Can these bones live?" Reflect about whatever comes to mind. Take time later to contemplate the questions in Further Reflections and the Bible verses below.

Can these bones live?

Further Reflections

1. What in your life (a relationship, a goal or situation) has died, or is on life support? Ask God if he desires you to speak life to it, or is he perhaps breathing new life somewhere else?

2. Have you experienced the breath of God firsthand? If you want the spirit of God, or more of the spirit, start by asking God to remove anything that might be blocking it. Ask for it; call for it; wait for it.

Lectio Divina

John 3:5-8

"I tell you the truth; no one can enter the kingdom of God unless he is born of water and Spirit. Flesh gives birth to flesh, but the Spirit gives birth to Spirit. You should not be surprised at my saying, 'You must be born again.' The wind blows wherever it pleases. You hear its sound, but you cannot tell where it comes from or where it is going. So it is with everyone born of the Spirit."

Luke 15: 22-24

But the father said to his servants, "Quick! Bring the best robe and put it on him. Put a ring on his finger and sandals on his feet. Bring the fattened calf and kill it. Let's have a feast and celebrate. For this son of mine was dead and is alive again; he was lost and is found." So they began to celebrate.

Chapter 37

Have you any right to be angry?

But Jonah was greatly displeased and became angry. He prayed to the Lord, "O Lord, is this not what I said when I was still at home? That is why I was so quick to flee to Tarshish. I know that you are a gracious and compassionate God, slow to anger and abounding in love, a God who relents from sending a calamity. Now O Lord, take away my life for it is better for me to die than to live." But the Lord replied, "Have you any right to be angry?"

Jonah 4: 1-4

But God said to Jonah, "Do you have any right to be angry about the vine?"

"I do," he said. "I am angry enough to die."

Jonah 4:9

We are not told very much about the prophet Jonah. His book is just four chapters long, and he only had one mission—to go to the wicked kingdom of Nineveh and give them an ultimatum: *repent or be destroyed.* When God tapped Jonah to go to Nineveh, it was the last thing he wanted to do. Others had argued with God, were reluctant about their commission, or lacked confidence to do it, but Jonah was the only one who ran away. He hopped a ship and went in the opposite direction.

While at sea a storm came up. Jonah confessed to the sailors that the storm was probably God's doing since he was running away from him, so, wanting to appease an "angry god," they threw Jonah overboard. Then the big fish swallowed him up, and finally "saved" him by spewing him out three days later onto dry land.

(There's a lot to learn here about running away from God and what can happen when we do—what storms will come our way, and how our salvation can look like a calamity, but now on to God's questions.)

The whole episode at sea convinced Jonah that God would not tolerate his running away again, so he went to Nineveh without a shred of enthusiasm and, in spite of his reluctance, preached to the Ninevites. They listened, they believed God's message, and they repented. Every person in the kingdom, including the King, humbled himself, fasted, and called with amplified urgency on the Lord. Just as Jonah suspected, the Lord had compassion and forgave them, which was God's desire and Jonah's fear all along.

Jonah was outraged. He did not want the Ninevites to repent because he knew God would forgive them, and he didn't want them forgiven or provided a second chance. His basic prayer to God: "I knew this would happen—I knew you would let them off the hook. How could you forgive them! Take me now—I don't even want to live."

Then God said to Jonah, "Have you any right to be angry?"

Jonah did not even respond. He went outside the city to pout.

Jonah thought he had every right to be angry. God had offended his sense of justice. The further implication is that God didn't see it that way at all. You get the sense that Jonah wished the Ninevites would sin again so he could say to God, "I told you so." Imagine his thoughts: "God, these people were really evil and you did not punish them, but you've punished my people many times. Evil requires punishment or there's no justice. What were you thinking?"

Because God forgave these wicked people, Jonah judged him for not being just or righteous. Their repentance was irrelevant to Jonah. He thought he was in the morally superior position vis-a-vis God. He thus justified his anger.

We all like the compassion of God and the grace of God when it's for us or one of our tribe. What about the grace shown to an outsider? Someone we might be jealous of, someone who hasn't paid his dues, or even worse, a rival or an enemy?

The question to all of us: what is our response when God shows compassion to the undeserving, not "one of us" but that "other" person who is undeserving? What is our response when God expects us to be his messenger to our nemesis, and we know he wants to forgive and bless him? What is our reaction when we suspect God does not treat us as equals?

Jesus taught his followers a parable about this kind of resentment. A landowner hired day laborers to work in his vineyard and agreed to pay them a denarius at the end of the day. Throughout the day, including up to the last hour of work, he hired worker after worker. Then he paid them all the same amount.

Naturally the ones who had toiled all day expected to make more than the latecomers and were angry when they didn't. They resented the latecomers, criticized the unfairness of the landowner, and thought they had a "right" to more money.

And who doesn't identify with them? Jesus ended the parable explaining who had the "rights" in this scenario: "I want to give the man who was hired last the same as I gave you. Don't I have the right to do what I want with my own money? Or are you envious because I am generous?" (*Matthew 20:14-15*).

In God's eyes, he had an opportunity to be generous to the sinners of Nineveh, just like the landowner in the parable had an opportunity to be generous to the workers who arrived at the last hour. The generosity of God, for "foreigners" or the "undeserving" in our own neighborhoods, can be a problem for us until we learn to be lavish in our own generosity, and that usually does not happen until we recognize and receive the lavish grace of God.

The second time God asked Jonah if he had a right to be angry was a different scenario. As mentioned earlier, after the Ninevites repented and God forgave them, Jonah retreated outside the city gates. While he sat in the hot sun, God caused a vine to grow and provide shade. Then the next day he caused the vine to wither. Jonah got mad *again*. God asked *again*, "Do you any right to be angry about the vine?"

This time Jonah answered the question. "I do," he said. "I am angry enough to die."

In the short time Jonah enjoyed the vine, he developed an attachment to it and was angry when it dried up. God enacted a living parable about a vine that was here one day and gone the next in order to demonstrate something. Jonah's reaction to losing the vine showed how much God cared about and had a "right" to his "vine," the Ninevites.

Another implication occurs with this second question—it has to do with our sense of entitlement. In very short order we become attached to our comforts and perks. When we lose them, we can get furious and look for someone to blame. Jonah believed the vine was "his" vine and was very upset when it withered. His attitude: "How dare you take away my vine!"

God pointed out that Jonah cared about a vine that shaded him for only one day. Could Jonah not comprehend how much God cared about the Ninevites? In this sense they were his vine.

God had just delivered a great city. Thousands of lives were saved, children were spared. Even the cattle were spared. Instead of rejoicing, Jonah felt resentful and angry. He nursed his rights. We love to be right and we love to cling to the upper hand with our "rights," but our anger can disable us from sharing God's mercy and compassion.

None of this makes us happy, it doesn't even make us right. It just gives us the illusion of being right. When we cling to our rights to justify our anger, we find ourselves sitting in the seat of Jonah, and at cross purposes to God.

Prayer

Father,

I want a great heart. Teach me your ways. Conform me to the image of your Son. Help me to recognize and lay down my "rights" and entitlements. They are illusions anyway. Clothe me with your very own love and compassion.

And thank you for your great grace that includes me.

Amen

Settle down in the presence of the Lord and meditate on this question. "Have you any right to be angry?" Reflect about whatever comes to mind. Take time later to contemplate the questions in Further Reflections and the Bible verses below.

Have you any right to be angry?

Further Reflections

1. When have you squandered days or even weeks in anger over losing something you had a "right" to? Did you really have a right? Angry feelings are not always sinful, so when do you think you do have the right to be angry?

2. Have you ever been critical of grace given to someone you don't like?

Lectio Divina

Psalm 86:15
> But you, O Lord, are a compassionate and gracious God,
> Slow to anger, abounding in love and faithfulness.

Matthew 5:44-45
> But I tell you: Love your enemies and pray for those who persecute you that you may be sons of your Father in heaven. He causes his sun to rise on the evil and the good, and sends rain on the righteous and the unrighteous.

James 2:13
> Judgement without mercy will be shown to anyone who hasn't been merciful. Mercy triumphs over judgement.

Chapter 38

Should I not be concerned about that great city?

But the Lord said, "You have been concerned about this vine, though you did not tend it or make it grow. It sprang up overnight and died overnight. But Nineveh has more than a hundred and twenty thousand people who cannot tell their right hand from their left and many cattle as well. Should I not be concerned about that great city?"

Jonah 4:11

The book of Jonah is about God saving a corrupt (but repentant) nation that he cared about deeply. It is also a story about the great lengths God will go to for just one man, an angry man that God also cared about very much. God knew who Jonah was; he didn't make a mistake in choosing him. Jonah was not just a pawn God used. God cared about Jonah, too.

Look at the trouble God went to for this man who not only ran away but argued with him about saving a city that God called "great." God could have chosen another messenger at any time, so we can assume he had a reason for choosing Jonah. Here's the sequence of events:

God called Jonah to give a message to the Ninevites. Jonah ran away as fast and far as he could.

1. While at sea the Lord caused a great storm and the sailors threw him off the ship. God sent a big fish to swallow him and deliver him to dry land.
2. Jonah went to Nineveh and delivered the message. The Ninevites repented and God spared them. After which—
3. Jonah retreated in anger. God showed up and asked why he was angry.
4. Jonah, still mad, went off by himself. God caused the vine to grow and the vine to wither.
5. God sought Jonah again.

In the whole story Jonah showed some heart and some

faith only one time. From the belly of the fish, when his life was on the line, he prayed:

> Those who cling to worthless idols forfeit the grace that could be theirs.
> But I, with a song of thanksgiving, will sacrifice to you. What I have vowed, I will make good. Salvation comes from the Lord.
>
> *(Jonah 2:8-10).*

What happened to this faith? God sought Jonah nonstop. He saved his life. As soon as Jonah turned toward God while he was in the belly of the fish and facing certain death, God "delivered" him onto dry land. Jonah experienced God's grace in a profound way. Why would Jonah resent this same saving grace offered to the Ninevites, who also turned toward God?

In the end, this story is not just about the Ninevites and Jonah. It's also a story about God's great heart. "Nineveh has more than 120,000 people who cannot tell their right hand from left and many cattle as well. Should I not be concerned?" *(Jonah 4:11).*

A whole city of lost people, and many cattle. God cared about them all. Jonah's rebellion came close to disrupting the great salvation God had planned for the Ninevites. Furthermore, Jonah's anger robbed him of the joy of the moment, the joy of being in cahoots with God, the privilege of playing a special role in this adventure.

In the hope it would touch his heart, perhaps God said gently to Jonah, "Should I not be concerned about this great city?"

Centuries later, Jesus showed this same compassion to

Jerusalem. He yearned to gather the whole city to him. He poured out love to undeserving people and offended the "deserving" who believed he made a big mistake even to speak to the riff-raff. He came to seek and save what was lost. He might as well have said that he came to save people who didn't know their right hand from their left.

The love and affection of God are precious gifts. The self righteous just can't seem to receive them and they would deny them to anyone not as "righteous" as they are.

The subject of self-righteousness and grace was a theme in the movie *Philomena*, set in Ireland. When Philomena was young and pregnant she had been sent to a home run by nuns. They shamed her, abused her and, against her will, sold her baby to wealthy Americans. Fifty years later, after a quest to find her child, she discovered he had died a few years before. She had every right to be angry.

In the last scene of the movie, Philomena confronted the one nun still alive from those earlier bitter days. Sister Hildegard was a very old woman by then but still full of judgment, bitterness, and self-righteousness. Philomena told her she forgave her.

In the movie, you don't see this grace coming, and it is quite powerful. By this scene, everyone hates Sister Hildegard. But Philomena, who had a "right" to hate her, forgives her.

It's so hard for us to see that God is concerned with Philomena *and* Sister Hildegard.

We want clear delineations between good and bad. We want rewards and punishments.

But God pours out his love and invites us to change our minds and our lives and join him. God pours out his grace on the undeserving Ninevites, and on undeserving Israelites, on the thief who died beside Jesus, on Saul who persecuted the disciples of Jesus, and on undeserving Jonah.

Jonah's story requires us to consider two more questions: Who deserves God's abounding love? Who deserve his forgiveness?

We don't know if God's last appeal to Jonah moved his heart or if he remained stuck in his anger like Cain, the first man God spoke to about his anger. Maybe he softened; maybe it would take years for him to lay down his anger, or maybe he never would. In the belly of the fish, Jonah had declared that those who cling to worthless idols forfeit the grace that could be theirs.

An idol is not always a foreign god; it can also be a god of our own design. Jonah could not see that he clung to an idol. He worshipped a god of justice without mercy, (in spite of repentance). He was the one who forfeited God's grace.

At least one lesson for us is this: when we contemplate someone who has done something really bad, we need to listen for God's voice deep in our heart asking, "Should I not be concerned about them?"

Prayer

Father,

I read the story of Jonah and think what a great adventure. I don't understand why he was so resentful. Please show me anytime I'm veering into resentment, because I don't want to miss out on any adventure with you. I want to be in on what you are doing in the world. I want to be like you, gracious, slow to anger and abounding in love. I want all of us to receive your amazing grace with great joy.

Thank you for inviting me to play a part.

Amen

Settle down in the presence of the Lord and meditate on this question, "Should I not be concerned about this great city?" Reflect about whatever comes to mind. Take time later to contemplate the questions in Further Reflections and the Bible verses below.

Should I not be concerned about this great city?

Further Reflections

1. Think of someone really unlikeable or someone who really doesn't like you. How do you feel about the great compassion God has for that person? Do you think if you knew more of their story you might feel compassion, too?

2. Have you ever run away from God? Are you still running? How has that worked out?

Lectio Divina

Matthew 12:41
"The men of Nineveh will stand up at the judgement with this generation and condemn it; for they repented at the preaching of Jonah, and now one greater than Jonah is here."

Luke 13:34
"O Jerusalem, Jerusalem, you who kill the prophets and stone those sent to you, how often I have longed to gather your children together, as a hen gathers her chicks under her wings, but you were not willing!"

Psalm 145:8 (The Passion Translation)
> You're kind and tenderhearted to those who don't deserve it
> And very patient with people who fail you.
> Your love is like a flooding river overflowing its banks with kindness.

Chapter 39

Who despises the day of small things?

Then the word of the Lord came to me: "The hands of Zerubbabel have laid the foundation of this temple; his hands will also complete it. Then you will know that the Lord Almighty has sent me to you."

"Who despises the day of small things?"

Zechariah 4:10

King Cyrus has at last released the people of Judah, held captive by Babylon for 70 years, and some have returned home. Zechariah the prophet was with this first wave. When they got home, they found Jerusalem and their temple demolished. This ragtag group of refugees was supposed to rebuild it all, but it was rubble (think Mosul after Iraq defeated Isis). Just clearing the debris must have seemed insurmountable. They were about to lose heart and give up.

Then the Lord spoke encouraging words to Zechariah. "Who despises the day of small things."

Zechariah knew they were overwhelmed. He was, too, but God showed him a vision of what Jerusalem would become, and he in turn told everybody what he saw: the streets of Jerusalem were filled with people, old and young alike. The girls and boys laughed and played. Visitors went to the temple and prayed to the Lord.

As he spoke, the builders worked. Their confidence grew. They built the wall in record time. In fact, they rebuilt the wall so fast that they convinced the surrounding naysayers that God was indeed with them. Then they went on to rebuild the temple.

Sometimes when we start to build or rebuild something, the first task is to clear the rubble, or at least the rubble in our own minds and hearts. Sometimes we have to deal first with the mess we or someone else has made, or what we ran away from or left unfinished. Sometimes the small thing is to overcome our own paralysis.

That first step may feel so insignificant. When much effort

only makes a dent in the job to be accomplished, it can feel overwhelming. Moving debris does not seem important. Despair can set in. The returning Israelites could have given up before they made any real progress. And so can we: on a job, a marriage, a child, a life.

This story in Zechariah begins with the aftermath of devastation. I can't help but think about the shocking images from 9/11 and remember the first responders. I also have several close family members who live in Houston and survived hurricane Harvey. (Almost everybody who lives in Texas knows somebody who survived hurricane Harvey.) Again there was immense destruction, but we also watched volunteers from all over Texas and Louisiana pouring forth in those early days of "small beginnings." In both cases, the city that was desolated was, after a time, made beautiful and thriving once again.

Havoc can wreck our personal lives, too. God sees the first day following the break-up of the marriage you did not see coming and did not want. I think he cheers even if all you can do is make the bed. He sees the girl who was abused, whose "walls" were violated, and as a result she became vulnerable to wicked people.

God cheers her, too, when she resurrects her boundaries—one "No" at a time. He sees the widow the day after the funeral, the day she begins the lonely journey of grieving the life that's over and building the new life to come. Surely we face as many hazards in building, and then rebuilding, our lives as the returning Israelites faced in rebuilding Jerusalem.

"Who despises the day of small things?"

God posed this question as he poured out promises that the temple would be rebuilt and that everyone would rejoice, that

Jerusalem would be full of happy families. The question had the answer built in: God loves, in fact, he honors the day of small things.

The first small steps can lead to something grand. Between the big turning points of our lives, many of our days seem small, just ordinary days to get through. But when God sees the day of small things, he sees the beginning of a great work.

My children now rear their own children and often their days are full of small things— changing diapers, doing laundry, school drop-offs, trips to the doctor's office, dinner, and bedtime stories. They work outside the home, too, so their days include the commute, the job, grocery shopping, cooking meals, cleaning up, and taking out the trash.

Here's what I see. They are establishing themselves as parents; they are creating secure, harmonious environments for their children. The very ordinary routines communicate a rhythm of peace and security.

On the face of it, these are days of small things, but they are also building something huge and important. These trivial, ordinary activities embrace a holiness. If only we could see the temple we are building with our lives in all these small things.

One more thought.

The first task the returning captives had was to rebuild the city wall. It wouldn't do to build the temple or new homes while they were still vulnerable to their enemies. So in the project of building your life, it's a good idea to pay attention to your own security and the places where your walls may have been desecrated, leaving you exposed.

All these days of small things count. God sees you in all your messiness and in your glory, and "he will rejoice over you with singing" (*Zephaniah 3:17*). If you now face the first day of a massive undertaking and you feel overwhelmed, take heart. God loves baby steps.

Prayer

Lord,

I actually love to be the cheerleader, the one cheering on my family, my children, my husband, nieces and nephews, and my friends. I love to catch a glimpse of the work you are doing, the project you have in mind, and search out your very own encouraging words.

Thank you that you are bigger than all my circumstances. My problems are not problems to you.

Thank you that you call me to sit beside you at the times I feel overwhelmed, that you welcome me every time I need to know that you love me, too.

Thank you for cheering me on.

Amen

Settle down in the presence of the Lord and meditate on this question, "Who despises the day of small things?" Reflect about whatever comes to mind. Take time later to contemplate the questions in Further Reflections and the Bible verses below.

Who despises the day of small things?

Further Reflections

1. Think of two goals you would like to undertake, one physical, one spiritual. What small step can you take this week or incorporate into your daily routine to facilitate these goals?

2. When and where has an enemy ransacked the sacred places of your heart? What steps could you take to begin your restoration?

Lectio Divina

Luke 19:17
"Well done, my good servant!" His master replied. "Because you have been trustworthy in a very small matter, take charge of ten cities."

Psalm 74:3
Turn your steps towards these everlasting ruins, all this destruction the enemy has brought on the sanctuary.

Isaiah 58:12
Your people will rebuild the ancient ruins and will raise up the age-old foundations; you will be called Repairer of Broken Walls, Restorer of Streets with Dwellings.

Chapter 40

What do you see, Jeremiah?

Then the Lord asked me, "What do you see, Jeremiah?"

Jeremiah 1:11, 1:13, 24:3
Amos 7:8, 8:2
Zechariah 4:2 and 5:2

"What do you see?" This was one of God's favorite questions. He repeated it many times to many different prophets, at least seven, by my count. Sometimes what the prophets saw was fantastic, other times it was quite ordinary. A prophet might "see" something and God would follow up with another question and a dialogue about the vision.

Other times the prophet seemed to be minding his own business when the Lord (or one of his angels) showed up and asked the question out of the blue. Then the prophet would look (with inner or outer vision) and describe what he saw. Each vision was packed with meaning and messages. They were often riddles and had to be pondered.

The first time God asked Jeremiah what he saw was right after God called him to be his prophet. Jeremiah was young and, like others before him, he was not certain he was ready for the job. When God asked him the question, he wanted to show Jeremiah that he really *could* "see" things. That he was ready. Jeremiah answered the question, "I see the branch of an almond tree" (*Jeremiah 1:11*).

Here's the explanation. The almond tree was the first tree to bloom or "wake up" in the spring. The Lord thus assured Jeremiah that he (the Lord) would watch over (be wakeful and alert) to the words he would tell Jeremiah to say. He gave assurance he would make them come true, or bear fruit, just like the almond tree.

This was not a big vision, it wasn't a message to any nation, and it wasn't nearly as strange as Ezekiel's vision of the dry bones. It was intimate, just between God and Jeremiah. It was another way of assuring Jeremiah he was the man God had chosen, he could see correctly, that God would be with him, and the Lord would be the one to make things happen. Jeremiah's job was to tell the people what God told him. God would watch over the whole enterprise.

The Lord later showed Jeremiah two baskets of figs, one ripe and tasty, the other bad and inedible, then he said, "What do you see, Jeremiah?"

He answered, "Figs."

God then explained the significance of the vision: The good figs were the good "sheep," now in exile, which God promised to watch over, protect, and in time bring back to Judah. The bad figs were the king and officials who had led the sheep astray to begin with, mostly by installing other gods and worshipping them. These faithless leaders would be banished from the Promised Land forever.

The figs could have been a mental picture that Jeremiah saw in the context of seeking God through prayer, a mystical vision, or two physical baskets of figs God used at that moment to speak to him. The amazing thing is that Jeremiah could perceive what God pointed out to him, and he could hear God's voice, audible or inaudible, explaining, warning, encouraging, or consoling.

God also asked Amos and Zechariah what they saw. What they saw was often ordinary but laden with symbols. Amos saw a bowl of bad fruit. Zechariah saw a gold lampstand and two olive trees. Each of them had to get an explanation for what these things meant.

Neither saw the point at first. The Lord clarified.

The vision of overly ripened fruit meant that the time for

judgment of Israel was ripe. The vision of the gold lampstand and olive trees was more complicated, but God also spelled out to Zechariah what it meant: the returning Jews would rebuild the city "not by might, nor by power, but by my Spirit" (*Zechariah 4:6*).

The prophets knew God could show up anytime. They knew he often spoke to them in symbolic language, in pictures, visions, and dreams. The visions became signposts of what God was doing and where he was leading. Prophets needed to be on alert so as not to miss an encounter with God.

We have no reason to believe God does not still communicate with us this way or he might not ask us the question, "What do you see?" God is not contained or restrained by how we think he will or should communicate with us.

These accounts fill the scriptures, so there is good reason to believe he still communicates this way. We have the Biblical canon, some may argue now, so God does not have to resort to visions anymore.

I wonder how God feels about that.

Many of us probably identify with Jeremiah—we're not sure we can "see" anything, much less figure out the deeper meaning of a dream or vision; but there's every reason for us to believe, just like God trained Jeremiah and gave him practice visions, he will do the same for us.

In fact, God asked me this very question. When I "looked," I saw smoke signals off in the distance.

Then he asked me, "What else?"

I "saw" a procession of people, far away, walking towards me. Somehow I understood—saw—that the vision meant that help was on the way. It was a message of hope I desperately needed at the time. God told me to come back in a year and,

"It will be done."

That year became a walk of faith. Here were some of the questions I had to work through: Was I imagining the whole thing? Was it really God? And if it was God, would he come through for me? Did I matter that much? Was he even concerned about our situation?

I dealt with a lot of anxiety over the circumstances but at last determined to resist fear and doubt, to trust him, to remember what I had "seen," and to take him at his word. In a year, it was done!

Help arrived in very unexpected ways. Out of the blue, a small investment from years before paid off, and new opportunities opened up.

I had worked as a lawyer representing families caught up in the Child Protective Services Department, but I hadn't done that work for a long time. I once again had that opportunity and I have represented these families ever since.

I also had the chance to do some real estate work again, which has always been fun for me. It's truly been a "procession of people" in my life since God's promise, and I've treasured every one. The vision didn't spell out any of this, but I felt God's presence and I learned to walk in the belief that help was on the way—and it was.

Our vision can be blurry, we focus on the wrong thing (like our unsolvable problems and how long they have persisted), or we might not take seriously a dream or vision God uses to communicate with us. Maybe, like the old prophets, we need to pay attention; we need to be on the look-out for those moments when God comes alongside us and whispers his questions.

All the questions God asked and all the conversations he held reveal something very important that we can miss in these postmodern times: how much God wants to communicate with us.

It's our turn to "see," like Jeremiah, Amos, Zechariah, and many others. We are the ones now who get to talk to him and answer his questions, receive encouragement and say "yes" to his assignments. We get to know and be known by this amazing God.

Prayer

Father,

You showed your prophets many astonishing things and you called them to important quests on your behalf. I am on call for you, too, so please give me eyes to see what you are doing and ears to hear you.

I want to understand all the ways you speak to me. I love it when your word leaps off the pages, and I grasp that it is your personal word to me. I love it when I see something in the spiritual realm.

Teach me how to see. Make me perceptive always to your spirit. Out of all the voices calling out to me, let me hear your voice every time.

Amen

Settle down in the presence of the Lord and meditate on this question. "What do you see?" Reflect about whatever comes to mind. Take time later to contemplate the questions in Further Reflections and the Bible verses below.

What do you see?

Further Reflections

1. Clear your mind with some relaxing deep breathing. Remember that you are in the presence of God. Ask him to draw near and to sanctify your imagination. What do you see? (Remember that this can take time.)

2. Have you had a vivid or recurring dream? Ask God what message he is communicating to you, then pay attention for awhile to what comes to mind, to what you see. If you are concerned about whether you are "seeing" clearly, check your visions against scripture to make sure you are on track.

Lectio Divina

Ephesians 1:18
I pray also that the eyes of your heart may be enlightened in order that you may know the hope to which he has called you, the riches of his glorious inheritance in the saints.

Joel 2:28
I will pour out my spirit on all people. Your sons and daughters will prophesy, your old men will dream dreams, your young men will see visions.

Luke 11:33
Your eye is the lamp of your body.

EPILOGUE

There are great themes running through scripture illustrated by the questions God asked. Before closing this book, I'd like to highlight two that seem particularly important:

1. What we see, and
2. God's relentless pursuit of his children.

There is an overarching meaning to the question of what we see; it is how we see. This has played a silent role in all the questions. In a way, it holds the questions together. Because our vision can be skewed and we can focus on the wrong things, we can be deceived.

In the beginning of the whole story, the serpent suggested to Eve that the forbidden fruit would "open her eyes." Eve then took another look at that tree and and thought what she saw was good. But it wasn't.

We can be blind to what is right in front of us and totally miss what God is doing or offering. We read the account of Hagar when she and Ishmael were about to die in the desert. After the Lord spoke to her, her "eyes were opened" and she spotted the well that had presumably been there all along. She had been too distraught before to even notice.

God showed the stars to Abraham, and he saw a multitude of descendants before he and Sarah had conceived one child. Joseph saw in a dream that he would rule over his brothers.

When he shared his dream, for some reason they didn't appreciate it at all, so they sold him into slavery. Years later, when his dreams came true, Joseph saw that what his brothers meant for evil, God meant for good.

Eight spies scoped out the Promised Land and saw giants they could never defeat. Two spies, Joshua and Caleb, saw a land flowing with milk and honey and an enemy they could surely conquer. Forty years later, they led God's people into that land.

The Israelite army saw the giant Goliath and shook in their boots. David saw victory—with a slingshot and the help of the Lord. Prophets saw the Lord seated on a throne, a field of dry bones come to life, the son of man coming in the clouds, a new heaven and a new earth.

In the New Testament, the Pharisees saw unclean sinners, but Jesus saw lost sheep. His followers saw a mustard seed. He saw a tree of faith. The Romans saw a crucified man. His disciples saw a risen Lord. Ordinary men and women saw angels, dreamed dreams, and beheld visions. Others remained blind. A vision of Jesus blinded Saul so he could at last see the glory of God.

What God shows us is compelling, but how we see him, ourselves, and our world is all important. How we look at the world, how we see our fellow man, determines the outcome of so much of our lives. Earnest, sincere people still sometimes need a vision check. Seeing and understanding what we see can lead to abundant life or death—in all sorts of ways.

Most important of all is how we see God. The good news of scripture is that God keeps showing up. This is the second pattern revealed in the questions he asked. He shows up when we are in the belly of a fish, lost in a desert, sitting alone in the hot sun, hiding out in the bushes or in a winepress, or when we cannot tell our right hand from our left.

Our stubbornness and pride, our anger, fear, and doubt do not stop his relentless pursuit, nor his kindness and patience. The stories and all the questions he asks reveal the persistent faithfulness of the God who loves us.

His determined search for us—and his questions—do not stop at the close of the Old Testament. God sends his son to search for the lost, both those who know they're lost and those who don't. Those longing for the love and kindness of God "see" Jesus, the one who welcomes them.

Others, especially some of the religious leaders, do not want what he offers. Jesus keeps asking the questions to teach us about God and about ourselves.

Finally the pursuit of God culminates in the crucifixion where Jesus opened his arms for the whole world. The promise given to Abraham, that his seed would one day be a blessing to all people everywhere, finally comes true. It is still an open promise for all of us who yearn to be found by God.

To end, please contemplate the following verses from the prophet Isaiah:

> I will go before you
> and will level the mountains;
> I will break down gates of bronze
> and cut through bars of iron.
> I will give you hidden treasures,
> riches stored in secret places,
> so that you may know that I am the Lord
> The God of Israel who summons you by name.
>
> *Isaiah 45: 2-3*

Acknowledgments

I am filled with gratitude for the people who have mentored me, taught me, prayed for me and with me. These are my spiritual fathers, mothers and friends:

Poozie Swann, Jill Ramey, Sally Stout, Father William Millsaps, Creath Davis, Malcolm Smith, Kelly Koonce, and Miriam Burke.

I'm exceptionally blessed and inspired by two extraordinary groups of friends, the Sunday night group and the "Art of Engaging Holy Scripture" Bible study at Good Shepherd Episcopal Church. Each one of you walks the walk.

I've shared the journey with spiritual sisters as well. I'm extremely thankful for my oldest friend Eugenia, and my very old friends Carrie, Katherine and Ginger, Cynthia, Barbie, Kay, and Helen. For over twenty years I have had two prayer partners who have encouraged me in this project every step of the way. My immense gratitude to Ann Huthnance and Betty Boon. It's never good when you're both out of town at the same time.

Many thanks to my first editor Patton Quinn, to Kathleen Niendorff, who encouraged me along the way, and especially to Cynthia Stone, my editor and now friend, and for Treaty Oak Publishers, who made this book happen.

My heartfelt thanks to Michael Quinn for always believing in me and cheering me on, and to Patton, Jacob, Mary Hammon, Paul, and Cece because I love you all to pieces.

Finally I'm grateful beyond measure for Edith Anne, Lulu, Birdie, Seamus, and Peter. Each of you is a grace in my life. May you all come to know how profoundly you are loved by our most loving God.

ABOUT THE AUTHOR

I grew up in Texas, graduated from UT Austin, and moved to Dallas to teach high school English. After a few years I enrolled at SMU to study counseling psychology. I completed a Master's degree at the same time I met and married my husband.

In Kansas City, where my husband attended law school, I worked at a small psychiatric hospital. We returned to Austin with our first child and I taught psychology as an adjunct professor at SMU, (among other jobs between the births of our next two children.)

I became interested in law and enrolled in school one more time. I graduated from SMU law school, worked for one year at a big law firm, and then left for a different kind of practice. For many years I represented juveniles at the Dallas Public Defender's office, did the same in private practice, and also took court appointments to represent parents or children caught up in Child Protective Services. I've continued that work to this day in Austin.

Paula Patton Quinn, *author*

I was raised in the Episcopal church, but have always participated in Bible study and prayer groups led by scholars, informal study circles in private homes, which often embrace intimate group prayer, and the practice of *lectio divina*. I also completed a two-year study of spiritual direction.

I'm still married (43+years) to my husband, Michael. Our three children are now grown and we enjoy the pleasure of five grandchildren.